Four Plays, Foreplay, For play

Four Comedies by

Art Mayers

Four Plays, Foreplay, For play

Acknowledgments

I would like to thank all the actors and production personnel that have indulged me in the production of these plays, Anne Dolan for fixing the typos, Joan Grant for the cover photo and Laura Billings for the back cover photo.

Art at the Lincoln County Weekly

Foreword

It was during the Q and A following the staged reading of *"Tournament"* at Emerson College as part of a Playwright's Platform presentation. The audience was beaming with enthusiasm. I was flanked by my wife and mother who were justifiably proud. It was my first step in becoming a recognized playwright. Then came the well-meaning question: "What are you going to do with this play, Mr. Mayers?" A one act straight play by a Maine based 30--year-old playwright had as much traction in the larger world as one of the 40,000 unsolicited screenplays that arrive in Hollywood every year.

So I set to work the only way I knew how, posting scripts to contests and trying to fall into the good graces of local community theater directors. I played bit parts from Brunswick to Belfast in hopes of attracting enough goodwill from directors that they might take a chance on one of my plays. The uniform answer was that the company or theater group had already set their schedule for the next two or more years but they would be happy to take a look. In most cases the directors failed to even return the scripts.

My next tack was to self produce. *"Open wide"*, the pre-cursor to "The History of Dentistry: part four". It was first performed in the Union Hall in Whitefield in the middle of winter. It took the wood furnace and a contractor's kerosene jet heater to keep the place warm for the duration of the show. We then toured to the Patten Free Library in Bath, where at intermission a friend performed a stand up comedy routine as an Oriental cook. Two of his friends came to heckle which freaked out my cast to the point where they did not want to return for the second act.

My next strategy was to build public confidence in my abilities by staging musical shows. Five musicals and 20 years later, *Renys: the Musical* was a local smash hit at the Waldo Theater in Waldoboro and later at the Lincoln County Community Theater in Damariscotta. With box office success I again returned to the straight plays. *"Tournament"* was restaged at LCCT as part of the Dead of Winter Players. That was followed by *"A Hand for Murder"* which shall appear in a later volume reserved for plays that tell stories that should be repeated but are bound not to amuse or entertain.

My personal and public credit was again stretched by my gall to produce plays of substance with a few laughs, but no music, I brought forward *"Mildred's Chorus"* in 2008. I had searched for years for a woman to play Mildred with no luck. I finally took the leap and publicized auditions with the hope of finding someone to play this challenging part. The woman I chose had a nervous breakdown a week before the show opened. At one in the morning I knocked on Ellie Hinds' door. We read the play, she took on the challenge and in five days stepped on the stage at the Waldo Theatre and made me proud.

"*Trading Up*" was produced in the 1980's by the Gaslight Theater in Hallowell, Maine as a staged reading. The play relies on rapid-fire dialogue which could not be sustained by actors with books in hand. Each of the four plays published here, I believe has weathered the test of time and could be restaged without appearing dated or diminished with current sensibilities. Please read and consider bringing them to life again.

Art Mayers

TABLE OF CONTENTS

Cast of " Gravel, Grovel, Gorilla" 1989

TOURNAMENT

Tournament was first performed in 1986 for Playwright's Platform at Emerson College as a staged reading. It was given a full staging in 2006 by the Dead of Winters Players at the Lincoln Community Theater in Damariscotta Maine.

Cast of characters (LCCT Cast)

Arnold 1……….. A quiet, chubby, 14-year-old boy, Luke Kalloch

Morris 1………… Arnold's father at 38, Dan True

Arnold 2………… Arnold 25 years later, Tom Handel

Morris 2………… Morris 25 years later, John Price

Arnold 3…………...Arnold 25 years after that , Kit Hayden

Morris 3…………….25 years after that, Art Mayers

The Cast of Tournament, 2006

SCENE ONE

The scene is set at a country club locker room and adjoining pro shop. This may be indicated with a row of lockers, a dressing bench, the club rack, a bucket of golf balls, maybe a poster and a few signs. The scene opens with the three Morrises lying prone on the dressing bench, stacked with the oldest on the bottom.

Morrises: (*In unison, apparently in pain*) Arnold! Son!

Arnolds: (*Converging from behind the exits or behind lockers in unison*) What is it, Dad?

Morris 1: The pain!

Morris 2: It's the grip.

Arnolds: What, Dad?

Morris 2: It's all in the grip.

Morris 1: You should always remember to tuck the pinky in.

Morris 3: It's your stance you should worry about.

Morrises: OHHHHH!

Arnolds: Dad!

Morrises: It's a great game, isn't it Arnold? (They go limp)

Arnold 1: (*Running out*) A doctor! Get a doctor!

Morrises: (*In spasms*) Nitros!

Arnolds 2 and 3: Nitros. Get the nitros. Where are the nitros?

Morrises: In the locker, Arnold.

Arnolds 2 and 3: (*Run to the lockers out of sight*) The lockers!

Arnold 2: (*Reappearing*) Which locker?

Morris 2: (*Pushing Morris 1 off of him to the floor and then rising slightly in order to direct traffic*)   Locker 34. Can't you remember anything, Arnold? My lucky number, 34.

Arnold 2: (*Ducking out of sight*) Right, Dad, 34.

Morris 2: No, Arnold! (*Arnold reappears*) That way! (*Arnold 2 exits in a given direction*)

Arnold 3: What's the combination, Dad?

Morris 3: (*Still prone as if in sleep*) 27 to the right, then left past zero to eight.

Morris 2: Nine! Can't you remember anything?

Morris 3: Past zero to nine.

Morris 2: Hurry, Arnold.

Arnold 2: (*Shaking the lockers*) I can't find the locker. I can't find 34.

Morris 2: What's wrong with you, Arnold? Can't you see I'm dying? (*Rises in disgust, exits in direction of Arnold 2*)

(Long pause).

Arnold 3: Well, Dad. Right to what? What's the last number, Dad?

Morris 3: That's not it. (*Slowly rising*) That's not it at all. I was not in the locker room. I was on the 14th green. (*Shuffles slowly to exit opposite Arnold 3*) How would you know, Arnold? You were in college. Or had dropped out. Besides it was my stance, not my grip. It was Eddie the Pro that saw the fall, face down on the green. He ran to me. I heard him ask me what was wrong. What's wrong, Mr. Morris? I said my stance. Not my grip. It was my stance that was killing me.

Arnold 3: Dad, what's the last number? Can you hear me? What's the last number?

Morris 3: (*At exit*) Don't you know anything, Arnold? 34. My lucky number. It was the stance, Arnold, not the grip, the stance. (*Exits*)

(*Long pause*)

Arnold 3: It won't open. (*Shakes locker*) It won't open! (*Continues to shake locker*)

Morris 1: (*Rises off the floor*) who is it? Who is it behind those lockers. Get out of here. Caddies aren't allowed in here. You should be helping Eddie. Smart alecks. (*Enter Arnold 1 carrying golf bag*) Get up before I call your boss. (*goes to the locker and opens it without difficulty*) Smart aleck kids. (*Arnold sets bags against the locker. They slide crashing to the floor*) Arnold, what's the matter with you? Are you awake yet? Were you doing this, sleeping in the car? (*Picking up the bags*) Why didn't you put these in the rack? They tend to stand up in the racks by themselves. If you don't want to wake up, we shouldn't be in this tournament. (*Stacking bags against each other*) This way they don't fall. Got it, Arnold? Son, Where is your duffel bag?

Arnold 1: I left it at home.

Morris 1: Arnold, where are your golf shoes?

Arnold 1: I can wear these.

Morris 1: Sneakers? You can't wear sneakers for a tournament. Arnold, this is the father and son tournament, not a driving range. You'll slip all over the place, son. Sneakers are for basketball.

Arnold 1: My cleats are too small.

Morris 1: Why didn't you say something, Arnold? You let things slide. You should have told me your cleats were too small?

Arnold 1: These are fine, Dad.

Morris 1: Don't be silly.(*Going to exit by push up and calling out*) Eddie! (*To Arnold*) Eddie is a fine pro and a great guy. Eddie wouldn't let his son play without cleats. Eddie!

Arnold 1: Eddie probably doesn't have a son.

Morris 1: Don't be a wise ass, Arnold. This is no time for jokes. Eddie! Eddie would cut his right arm off to help you Arnold. And he wouldn't let you slip on your ass in front of all the fathers and sons. Eddie!

Arnold 1: Can I wash the balls?

Morris 1: May I wash the balls?

Arnold 1: May I wash the balls?

Morris 1: I'm not worried about balls. Let's stick to the subject. The subject is cleats, Arnold, cleats that you forgot. Cleats that you failed to mention no longer fit. Cleats that might prevent a miserable day sliding on wet fairways. Go ahead, Arnold, wash the balls. Eddie? (*Exits to find Eddie. Arnold 1 exits carrying a handful of balls*)

Arnold 3:(*Shaking the locker*) 34, Dad? 34 is not working. (*Bangs again*)

Arnold 2:(*Enters with bag, hears banging, ducks behind the lockers*) Caddies! You don't belong here. Get out on the TV where you belong. Can't you read? Members only! No caddies! (*Emerges, goes to the locker, and sets down his pack*)

Morris 2: (*Enters slowly evidently suffering from his agent he. Sets his cloth bag down, which holds three or four clubs, against the locker. They fall over*)

6

Arnold 2: Dad! What the...(*He picks up the clubs*) You should leave the clubs in the racks.

Morris 2: I'm not an invalid, Arnold.

Arnold 2: Why carry excess baggage? It's a hot day.

Morris 2: There is always a breeze on the golf course.

Arnold 2: Why waste your energy? (*He changes into golf clothes*)

Morris 2: I have plenty of energy. I lack stamina. There is a difference, Arnold. You remember the time you shot the hole-in-one? 12th annual father and son tournament.

Arnold 2: I've never had a hole-in-one and neither have you.

Morris 2: Right on the fourth hole.

Arnold 2: You imagine things. Get dressed, Dad.

Morris 2: I've got the scorecard to prove it. I am dressed.

Arnold 2: Where are your golf clothes?

Morris 2: I'll show you when we get home. I saved the card. You were such a proud little bugger. Smile from ear to ear. I'll wear what I have got on, Arnold.

Arnold 2: That's a wool shirt. You can't wear a wool shirt. It's 88 in the shade.

Morris 2: That's what we shot, 88. Alternating shots, of course, we had a handicap. 88 on the first nine even with a hole-in-one. You were very inconsistent.

Arnold 2: Wool is a killer on a hot day. It doesn't breathe. Take one of my shirts.

Morris 2: We didn't do so well on the back nine.

Arnold 2: (*Offering a T-shirt*) Dad!

Morris 2: I'm not wearing alligators on my shirt. (*Arnold 3 shakes the locker out of sight*)

Arnold 2: (*Goes behind lockers as Morris 2 changes into T-shirt*) I told you caddies to get out of here!

Morris 1:(*Enters followed by Arnold 1*) I told you Eddie would come through for us. (Indicates a stack of shoes) There you go Arnold, pick your poison. Just put everything back the way it was. Well, what are you waiting for? You know your size?

Arnold 1: Nine.

Morris 1: We haven't got all day. (*Arnold goes about picking out shoes while Morris 1 goes to his bag and removes a club*) Remember, Arnold, to leave adequate time for warm-up. That includes practice swings. (*Takes out a wiffleball and places it on the floor*) Remember your fundamentals. Your stance, left till out right foot perpendicular to the line of flight. Ball should be just inside your heel with the woods...

Arnold 1: Dad, I've been playing for five years.

Morris 1: I know, Arnold. Five years is nothing. There is no substitute for sound fundamentals. Just like Ben Hogan says...

Arnold 1:(*Simultaneous with above*) Just like Ben Hogan says...

Morris 1: No tassels, Arnold. Your mother can't stand tassels.

Arnold 1: They've only got one size 9.

Morris 1: They only have one nine?

Arnold 1: They only have one 9 and it's got tassels.

Morris 1: Remember your grip, Arnold. You've got to interlock your pinky with your left index finger. Just bring your right index finger over and pointed down the shaft. Hogan and Boomer agree on this to the letter. You have a checklist for your grip, don't you Arnold? All golfers have a mental checklist for the grip.

Arnold 1: These are too small.

Morris 1: All golf shoes fit tight at first.

Arnold 1: They hurt me.

Morris 1: Try the tassels on. We'll tell your mother it was the only pair in your size.

Arnold 1:These are the tassels. They are the only pair in my size.

Morris 1: Walk around in them. (*Arnold does, wincing at every step*) They will break in after a few holes. The leather is always stiff. Stop making those faces.

Arnold 1: They hurt.

Morris 1: Tell me, Arnold, where do they hurt? Don't just say they hurt, that tells me nothing. Be specific.

Arnold 1 In the heel, and the toe... In the sides.

Morris 1: Don't exaggerate. Where do they hurt the most?

Arnold 1: All over.

Morris 1: That is no help, Arnold. (*Arnold starts to remove the shoes*) What are you doing? Keep them on, Arnold. You don't want to ruin the day, do you? Because if you plan to wear those old sneakers and you end up slipping and falling in front of everyone, that will ruin our day. You will ruin it for you, for me and for your mother who wants us to do well, to finish near the top of our age group and handicapping. Do you understand, Arnold? Think it over for a minute, Arnold. (*Takes a swing which is awkward and herky-jerky in the extreme*) Nothing like the fundamentals. Percy Boomer rode it out 20 years ago and nothing has changed.

Arnold 1: Who was Percy Boomer?

Morris 1: Just the greatest scientist of the game of golf of all time. Hogan is good for power, but Boomer knew a golf swing and could explain it in everyday words.

Arnold 1: Did he win anything?

Morris 1: Boomer was a golfer's golfer.

Arnold 1: Did he win the PGA?

Morris 1: The shoes, young man. Stop stalling. Well?

Arnold 1: I'll wear them.

Morris 1: That's my boy. How much are they? On the side of the box.

Arnold 1: (*Looks on box*) $67.50.

Morris 1:(*Rushing to grab a box*) Let me see that. Eddie! This place is going to the dogs. (*Exits carrying box followed by Arnold 1 grimacing at every step*)

Arnold 2: (*Re-enters from behind lockers, picks up a club and takes several practice swings just in the same style as Morris 1.Meanwhile Morris 2 has taken a large jar of nitroglycerin pills and is filling small vials which he places at every pocket and pouch and available in his golf bag. Arnold 2 stops and observes him*) What's up, Dad?

Morris 2: Stale. The nitros get stale. They lose their punch.

Arnold 2: Warm-up, Dad. Archie and his father will be along any time.

Morris 2: I am warm. I don't need to warm up.

Arnold 2: You don't want to pull something.

Morris 2: I don't worry about pulling muscles. What's your boss's father's name?

Arnold 2: Mr. Sloan.

Morris 2: How old is he?

Arnold 2: Archie said 85.

Morris 2: What do I call him, Mr. Sloan?

Arnold 2: Come on, Dad, at least do some stretches.

Morris 2: He's 85. Let him warm-up. An old duffer.

Arnold 2: He's not an old duffer. He's spry for his age.

Morris 2: No one 85 is spry. He is lucky his legs work at all. I don't want to be responsible for him.

Arnold 2: Archie's father is a healthy, spry, older man.

Morris 2: With one foot in the grave.

Arnold 2: His heart is fine.

Morris 2: How do you know?

Arnold 2: I know.

Morris 2: He's not using our cart.

Arnold 2: Archie's father walks. He carries his own bag.

Morris 2: A half arsenal.

Arnold 2: A full bag of clubs with three leather pouches, a towel, and an umbrella.

Morris 2: Those metal umbrellas are dangerous. You wouldn't catch me with a metal umbrella on the golf course in a thunderstorm. He is not hitching rides on our cart. I don't care how winded and pale he looks. He starts on foot, he stays on foot. I have enough problems without an old duffer dropping dead on the third tee. If he does, I'm playing on without him. He's not using my nitros either.

Arnold 2: Your angina hasn't bothered you in years.

Morris 2: But I can't pee. Pain is nothing. Pain I can deal with. It's trying to pee and not being able to.

Arnold 2: Go in the bushes.

Morris 2: I go into the bushes, but I can't pee there. I find a lot of golf balls but I can't pee. I don't want any 85-year-old man with a good prostate riding on my cart and following me into the bushes on every shot to watch me perform. Golf is a hard enough game without that.

Arnold 2: Whatever you do, don't talk about the stock market. Archie hates to talk about the stock market.

Morris 2: He is a broker?

Arnold 2: He's an investment counselor.

Morris 2: I'll talk to the old duffer.

Arnold 2: Do me a favor and talk about the weather.

Morris 2: It's hot. What's there to talk about?

Arnold 2: Just play golf and keep your mouth shut. (*They exit carrying bags*)

Morris 1: (*Enters, picks up the two bags. Looks in Arnold 1's bag. Removes a club. Examines it by holding it out in front of him*) Arnold! Get in here. On the double! (*Arnold 1 hobbles in, removes his shoes and puts on his old sneakers while:*) Look at this, Arnold. This club is bent. How can you play with these old twisted sticks? (*Goes and takes a club out of his own bag*) Look, Arnold.

Arnold 1: Big Boomer.

Morris 1: After Percy Boomer.

Arnold 1:(*together with above*) Percy Boomer.

Together: The greatest golfer who ever wrote a book.

Arnold 1: I know. I know. Boomer is your club. Custom made.

Morris 1: Take it, Arnold. It wasn't made for the Hogan swing.

Arnold 1: I couldn't use Big Boomer. It is yours.

Morris 1: We'll go with the sneakers. Try it. (*Arnold 1 takes a swing*) It is made for your swing. This is going to be our day, Son. I can feel it. (*Arnold runs out*) Where are you going?

Arnold 1: The ball washer.

Morris 1: Forget that, Arnold. What about Big Boomer? Arnold, we are late. Arnold, forget about washing the balls. (*Picks up the clubs and exits*) You want everything your way, don't you, Arnold? (*Exits forgetting Big Boomer*)

Arnold 3:(*From behind the lockers*) It won't open. Call a caddie. Call anyone.

Morris 3: (*Re-enters slowly, watches the Big Boomer, picks it up*)

Arnold 3:(*Re-enters opposite*) Dad, you're alive.

Morris 3: What did you think, Arnold? It's Big Boomer.

Arnold 3: You scared me.

Morris 2: I haven't had a heart attack in 30 years. I'm not starting again at my age. It's Big Boomer.

Arnold 3: Don't you remember, Dad? Big Boomer was a putter.

Morris 3: The hell it was.

(*Blackout*)

SCENE 2

(*Arnold 1 runs into the locker room, out of breath, concealing tears. He goes to his locker, pulls up the lock, pounds on locker door, slumps onto the bench head in hands, body heaving sobs. Enter Morris 1, carrying Arnold's driver. Morris 1 is angry and tries to conceal it without success. He props the driver against the lockers so that Arnold must see it if he were to look up*)

Morris 1: You dropped this. (*Pause*) Goddammit, you threw it. You were slipping, weren't you Arnold, slipping all over. That's what I told Eddie. We had to quit because you were slipping. (*Goes to the shoe rack*) What size is that? Nine? You want me to pick them out? What about tassels? What about the? Will you look over here for a minute, Arnold? (*Arnold looks*)

Arnold 1: I don't want any golf shoes. (*Puts his head back in his hands*)

Morris 1: You want to muff the ball the rest of your life? It's the law of physics, one of Newton's laws. You can't hit a golf ball if you can't grip the ground. Why don't you try t

...

Arnold 1: I don't want the shoes. (*Mumbling into his hands*)

Morris 1: Speak up so I can hear you.

Arnold 1: I don't want any golf shoes

Morris 1: You were swinging okay, Arnold. I was watching your sway.You may have been a little tight in the shoulders. You really beltedone on the first tee. That's not easy. Everyone watching you. Weshould have played your drive. Alternating shots means making choices.We made some bad choices. I can see why you topped the second shot.My ball was in the hole. It's all tufty over there on the right. That was up on that topic to the little hole. It really is very easy totop that kind of ball. You have to move a little closer to compensateand modify the arc of the backswing. You should have used a five iron not a three wood. That was my fault. I should have treated it likerough. So what, we were on the green in three. You have to remember that the course greens always putt slower than the practice green. They water them more. Never up, never in. We double-bogeyed the first,so what? Arnold, did you smack one on the second! That showed them.You did get under it a little. You really should use a shorter tee, son. I didn't think that ball would ever come down. A hundred yards up, eighty down the fairway. You should use a shorter tee. So we played my drive again. Is that so terrible? You really should be careful on the down slope, Arnold. You should choke up a little andadjust your stance. The natural tendency is to take a full swing andthe clubface is not ready and the ball slices off to the right. Liveand learn. The woods over there are so sick I had a clear shot tothe green. 10 feet from the cup. That second reading tends to get burned out in such a slope facing the sun. If you would remember just tap the ball on the down slope. Putting is a fine art in itself. I missed the 20-footer coming back. We are all human. Are you sleeping, Arnold?

Arnold 1: (*Shakes his head*)

Morris 1: What?

Arnold 1: No!

Morris 1: Because I'm not going through this for my benefit. It isn'tevery day that the son of mine throws his driver into the water hazard and walks off the course. I am looking for some answers, Arnold. (*Long pause*) If we want tassels we can have tassels, can't we, Arnold? (*Long pause*) You definitely slipped on the third tee. Again you are playingmy drive. Big deal. You don't need two good drives when you alternate shots. On the upslope you have to let out a little club and adjust the stance or the ball will pop off the toe of the club. If you only pay attention I wouldn't have to keep reminding you. Another double bogey on three. The fourth hole has always treated you well. Remember when you just missed the hole in one? This time we are both in the bunker.You came out good and clean, too clean. We're in the woods again. Behind a tree. I put us back in the sand trap, clearly my fault. If I told you once, I've told you a hundred times, when you want to get out of deep sand, you aim behind the ball. You seem to be deaf or asleepwhen you play. I certainly don't understand it. When you don't take sand, the ball is going to slam into the lip of the trap and Ben Hogan himself couldn't blast it out. Not with dynamite! (Sighs) We're out of the trap in four tries, and three putts for 11 on a par three where you once nearly got a hole in one. So what? Big deal! It's certainly no reason to throw a temper tantrum. Walking off the course. I don't care how many balls you drive into the water. I don't care whether it was a new ball. It was a cheap dollar ball from the goddam pro shop. There were more balls in the bag. There are certainly more balls in this bucket. (*He takes the bucket of balls, spills themon the floor*) Who cares how many balls to put in the pond? You don't have to lose your head about it.

Arnold 1: I don't want to talk about it.

Morris 1: What do you want to talk about? Sex? The weather? The stock market?

Arnold 1: I do not want to talk about it.

Morris 1: What, about being a bad sport? You want to talk about that?

Arnold 1 No! (*Rising*) I'm going to the car.

Morris 1: No, you don't yet, young man. Sit down, Arnold. (*He does*)

Arnold! What are we going to tell your mother?

Arnold 1: I don't care.

Morris 1: I don't care? When she asks me how we did. I don't care? Arnold, you really soured a very fine day.

Arnold 1: I hate it! I hate it! I hate it!

Morris 1: What do you hate? Golf? You like golf.

Arnold 1: I hate it! It's the stupid clubs. They are too long.

Morris 1: We will get new clubs.

Arnold 1: It isn't the clubs. The whole game is dumb. Walking aroundthe dumb field hitting a golf ball into a dumb hole. You hit the dumbball straight and the dollar ball goes right. You hit the dumb ball right and the dumb ball goes up in the air. You hit the dumb ball up and it dives into the dumb water. If you hit the ball good you have to wait for the dumb people. Wait for all the dumb people in front of you. If you go in the woods you let the dumb people from behind play through, then you wait for them waiting for the dumb people putting on the green. When do we ever get to play through?

Morris 1: You can't hit the ball all over the place and expect to play through.

Arnold 1: Just like I said, a dumb game. (*Pause*) I hit the ball.

Morris 1: You were inconsistent. If you would stick to fundamentals...

Arnold 1: I said I quit. I'm not playing that stupid game, wear these stupid shirts, and carry these stupid clubs around the stupid course. The whole game is stupid, stupid, stupid...

Morris 1:(*Sits down suddenly staring into space, frozen*) Arnold...

Arnold 1: What is it?

Morris 1: Go to the car. In the glove compartment. A little bottle. Hurry.

Arnold 1: Dad!

Morris 1: I'm okay, just go to the car. (*Arnold 1 runs out passingArnold 2 and Morris 2 entering. Morris 1 continues to stare out,breathing heavily, Morris 2 sits beside him and stares out in the same way*)

Morris 2: I'm okay, Arnold. Don't worry about me. I just need a breather.

Arnold 2: I told you to just forget about the lousy ball. I don't knowwhy you insist on looking for those old cracked balls in the rough. We could have played my drive.

Morris 2: Your drive was in a hole.

Arnold 2: Just a mild depression.

Morris 2: It was a goddam gully. I couldn't have gotten it out with a sand wedge.

Arnold 2: At least it was on the fairway.

Morris 2: Thirty feet off the tee. Your boss and his lousy father weretaking out their eight irons and we were hardly off the tee.

Arnold 2: At least the ball was in play, not across the road in a cow pasture

Morris 2: Not my fault I slice the ball.

Arnold 2: If you would warm up a little bit, you wouldn't slice the ball.

Morris 2: When do you expect me to warm up? With your boss and his octogenarian father jogging along like the Yale track team.

Arnold 2: I was willing to settle for a six on the first hole

Morris 2: As they say, never up, never in.

Arnold 2: So you whack at the ball and almost drive it off the green. And what was the idea of bending Archie's ears about the stock options?

Morris 2: Archie seemed interested.

Arnold 2: He wasn't.

Morris 2: He should be. I have money in pension funds.

Arnold 2: Archie doesn't handle pension funds. He does estates. Mostof his customers are planning for death or are dead already.

Morris 2: People on pension funds die too. I should know.

Arnold 2: What do you know?

Morris 2: I know that anyone who isn't interested in the March put inIBM isn't interested in money.

Arnold 2: Don't you understand? Our clients are not interested inshort-term gains. Most of our customers are dead.

Morris 2: That's no excuse for not making money.

Arnold 2: You were making Archie nervous.

Morris 2: He wasn't so nervous when he sank that birdie putt on the fourth.

Arnold 2: I know my boss. I know when my Archie is nervous.

Morris 2: That reminds me of Sam Snead in the Open. Snead is on thelast hole, match tied, he needs to sink the putt for the match. Justas he starts his stroke a dog runs out of the crowd, a St. Bernard,

and goes through his legs. He sinks the putt and his caddie runs out to shake his hand. " Boss, I was getting nervous when that dog ran between your legs." Snead turns to the caddie, "Was that a real dog?"

Arnold 2: You are changing the subject.

Morris 2: Everyone should be interested in options. Options are important. Archie seemed interested enough in my call on eBay when he was in the sand trap on the fifth. And on the sixth when he hooked into the rough he seemed interested enough in the December put on GE.

Arnold: And what was this waving to Archie on the seventh fairway?

Morris 2: I'm an old man. When people wave at me, I wave back.

Arnold 2: Archie was waving for you to shut up, so he could take hisshot. Archie doesn't want your opinions on the stock market, especially on his day off.

Morris 2: I have made studies.

Arnold 2: You have made studies. You should have been a scientist. Instead you crawled into your little closet and made a science out of every crap game in town. What is the point of an old man spitting blood to hit a ball like Tiger Woods?

Morris 2: I have never hit the ball better than I did today.

Arnold 2: But how long can you keep it up?

Morris 2: I still have my stock options.

Arnold 2: Another crap game. How much have you lost, really?

Morris 2: I'm learning every day.

Arnold 2: How much, Dad?Morris 2: That's the beauty of options. You play with nickels and dimes.

Arnold 2: How much?

Morris 2: I won't be a burden on you, if that's what you mean.

Arnold 2: That's not what I mean!

Morris 2: (*Suddenly staring into space*) Arnold, though to a locker.

Arnold 2: You've got your nitros. In your pocket.

Morris 2: My Isodil. In the locker. Hurry...(*Arnold 2 ducks behind lockers. Morris 3 enters at a snail's pace, sits down and stares out like Morris 1 and 2. Arnold 2 begins to shake the locker, out of sight*)

Morris 3: Goddam caddie. What the hell? (*Shaking stops. Arnold 3enters carrying a duffel bag*) Arnold, is that you? What's that,Arnold? Over there by the shower room? Arnold?

Arnold 3: That's a video game, Dad.

Morris 3: Oh? What's that?

Arnold 3:(*Goes to locker and starts combination*) Let's get to work,Dad. 27... eight. We have put this off too long. Directly right to34. You've been turning this lock for 50 years.

Morris 3: Couldn't be that long.

Arnold 3: You are 88 years old. 50 years of the same locker (*Opens the door*) and certainly smells like it. They should gold plate this lockerfor you. (*Starts to empty the locker*) Let's get it over with. Golf tees... scorecards... the ball with half a cover.

Morris 3: Dog got it. I ever tell you the story about Arnold Palmer?

Arnold 3: A thousand times. You want this? (*Holds out a soiled shirt*)

Morris 3: That's a good one. For polishing shoes. Remember that time when I bought you the golf shoes? You sat and cried because there weren't any tassels on them. Your mother hated tassels. She wouldn'tlet them in the house. We had to take them back. You were a cutelittle fella. You must have been five years old at the time. Bet you don't remember that far back.

Arnold 3: I remember things, Dad. I was 14 and...

Morris 3: You had an awful temper. You used to throw your clubs in thepond when things didn't go your way. Thank God you got over that. A bad temper and an athlete don't mix.

Arnold 3: Look. It's Big Boomer (Takes it out of the locker)

Morris 3: The hell it is.

Arnold 3: You remember when you gave it to me?

Morris 3: Big Boomer was a putter. An old wooden-handled putter. Idon't know what happened to it.

Arnold 3: Eddie cut it down for me. It was custom made.

Morris 3: But that isn't Big Boomer. Big Boomer was a putter.

Arnold 3: Dad, show me your old swing?

Morris 3: I haven't swung a golf club in 15 years and I don't want to start now.

Arnold 3:(*Handing it to him*) What the hell.

Morris 3: I have enough trouble standing on two feet.

Arnold 3: Take a half swing. You're not dead yet.

Morris 3: Give me that thing. If it was one thing I taught you it wasthe fundamentals. Ben Hogan. The greatest golfer of all time. He was a good teacher, too. That's what made him different. (*Takes a swing*)That wasn't half bad. Stand back. (*Swings again*). You never forget how

to hit a golf ball. (*He hands the club to Arnold*) Now keep your toe facing out.

Arnold 3: I know.

Morris 3: You're standing too far up on the ball.

Arnold 3: Dad, I know how to play golf.

Morris 3: Just turn your hand a little higher. Keep that pinky in, inmore! If you hold your pinky like that you'll hook it into the woods.The trouble with you Arnold is that you never listen. I tell you things and you take off and do it your own way. You never profited by the experience of others.

Arnold 3: You?

Morris 3: Me, Ben Hogan, Percy Boomer. You are just pigheaded. Now hold that pinky in, goddam it. (*Loses balance, collapses on bench*) Arnold, the locker!

Arnold 3: Dad!

Morris 3: In my locker.

(*Arnold 2 starts to shake the lockers again*)

Morris 1: Arnold, where are you?

Arnold 2: 27... eight... 34. Hurry, Arnold!

Morris 2: That's the wrong locker, Arnold. Locker 34.

Arnold 3: The locker is open, Dad.

Morris 1: Hurry, Arnold.

Arnold 1: I am hurrying, Dad.

Morris 2: Locker 34 not 44, Arnold, you dummy.

Arnold 3: The locker is open, Dad.

Arnold 2:(*Emerging from locker 34*) Why didn't you say so?

Morris 1, 2, 3: (*Together*) Arnold! (*They collapse against each other*)

Arnold 3: What happens now, Dad? I always wanted to know. For 50 years I've wanted to know. I remember we would walk together. Then you would stop and stare into space. A slight grimace, pain in your eyes, a tiny gasp, a frown. Everything would come to a stop, a frozen moment. What should I do? Run? Call for help? Was I responsible? How had I caused this? Had I walked too fast? Had I failed to pick up my room? How would I be held responsible? For what? And then everything was okay. The pain would pass. Oh, you would take thenitro. We would walk again but a little slower. We would come home early. Soon every time you stared I would stop, every time you frowned I would freeze, every time you stopped I would hold my breath. Waitingfor something. The death that never came. You had me. You were apiece of expensive pottery in my hands. My hands could never shake,never waver. Tell me, Dad. How does this end? How will this ever end?

Morris 1: (Coming out of stare) Arnold.

Arnold 1: Here, Dad, take your pills.

Morris 1: That's okay, Arnold. I'm okay now.

Arnold 1: Angina?

Morris 1: Just a little pain. That's all. It's over now. You were saying something? I'm sorry you aren't happy with golf. I thought you enjoyed golf.

Arnold 1: Golf is okay.

Morris 1: I suppose I could learn football.

Arnold 1: You are too old for football, Dad. Besides, you hate football.

Morris 1: I bet Eddie would let us pick up on the fifth... where we left off, so to say... to take a breather. I'll say you didn't feel well, okay?

Arnold 1: Okay.

Morris 1: We won't have to keep score you don't want to. Forget about the tournament. We'll just play a quiet round together, father and son, no scorecard.

Arnold 1: That's fine with me.

Morris 1: (They start to exit) What about Mother? Maybe we should keep the score just for Mother's sake.

Arnold 1: Okay, Dad.

Morris 1: Let's go, Son. (*They exit*)

Morris 2: 34, Arnold. 34 as in the combination, as in my lucky number,as in my age at the first father and son tournament. You were 10years old and cute as hell.

Arnold 2: I was 14 and you were 38.

Morris 2: Your clubs were so long, they nearly stuck you in the ribs. Two years later you got your first hole-in-one.

Arnold 2: I never shot a hole in one and neither did you.

Morris 2: Shall we pick it up where we left off? (*Rising*)

Arnold 2: Let's get going. It will be dark soon. (*They exit*)

Morris 3: So Palmer was on the green and a big dog runs between hislegs, a Dalmatian. So Tiger sinks his putt and then asked his caddiewhether it was a real dog. The caddie says, "Don't ask me, I'm only

the caddie." I thought I told you that one.

Arnold 3: What do you say we get some clubs and play a few holes?

Morris 3: I gave my clubs away.

Arnold 3: We could rent them. If we feel good, we could keep score. Ifwe get tired, we quit.

Morris 3: My edema. I'm not supposed to walk.

Arnold 3: We will get a golf cart.

Morris 3: What will Mother say?

Arnold 3: Mother's dead.

Morris 3: Hmmm. I thought it was me that was dead.

Arnold 3: What do you say?

Morris 3: It will kill me for sure.

Arnold 3: So what?

Morris 3: That's fine for you to say.

Arnold 3: You haven't had a heart attack in 30 years.

Morris 3: I haven't been playing golf either.

Arnold 3: You haven't been doing anything.

Morris 3: I don't have my nitros.

Arnold 3: (*Removes a bottle from the duffel bag*) Nitros! (*Goes to the locker, removes another bottle*) Nitros! (*Reaches in his own pocket*)Nitros ! Come on, I'll see if we can get set up with a bag.

Morris 3: You can't do that.

Arnold 3: Why not?

Morris 3: It's course rules. Two people can't play from the same bag.

Arnold 3: We are two old men, separated by one fact. You are myfather. Two old men can do what they want to do. I'll find the pro.

Morris 3: I don't have any golf shoes.

Arnold 3: So what?

Morris 3: I'll slip all over the place.

Arnold 3: So what? (*Exiting*)

Morris 3: I guess you're right. So what.

Blackout.

Trading Up

About the play

Trading up is the story of two widely different characters forged into one. Norman David Mayer was killed by police in front of the Washington Monument in December 1982 after threatening to blow up the monument to bring attention to nuclear disarmament. The other side of my Malcolm is a composite of my father and his broker friend, both in their 80s, who often made or lost more money through serendipity than by intention.

Trading up was given a staged reading by the Gaslight Theater in Hallowell, Maine in 1988.

Cast of characters

Helen Poop....... the receptionist

Dasher..............the heavy, Dartmouth '78

Asher.................not so bad, Dartmouth '78

Schlong.............a bit better, Dartmouth '78

Sitter.................really okay, Dartmouth '78

Malcolm Meyer.. the broker, 80

Ethel Meyer.......his sister

Earl....................the janitor

Anson Meyer..... the son

Dr. Beal.............the psychiatrist

SCENE ONE

Set to represent a brokerage house: desks, telephones business machines etc. Stage right, the receptionist. Stage left Malcolm Meyer is busy on the phones but separate from Asher, Dasher, Sitter and Schlong who sit at desks under travel posters, obviously not working.

Poop: Asher, Dasher, Sitter, Meyer, and Schlong. Mr. Asher? (*Asher looks up and shakes his head negative*) I'm sorry, Mr. Asher is in conference. Mr. Dasher? (*same routine*) I'm sorry Mr. Dasher is in conference. Mr. Schlong? (*Same*) I'm sorry, Mr. Schlong is in conference. Mr. Sitter. (*Same*) I'm sorry, Mr. Sitter is in conference. Mr. Meyer? Just a minute. Hello, Asher, Dasher, Siitter, Meyer and Schlong. (*All except Meyer shake their head that they are all out except Mr. Meyer*) Mr. Meyer, line 4.

Dasher: (*approaching Poop*) Hold all calls, Miss Poop.

Asher: (*dropping paper and addressing Schlong*) He's definitely too old. (*Indicating Meyer*)

Schlong: He's past retirement.

Sitter: Who is?

Asher: Who do you think?

Sitter: Dasher isn't 55 yet.

Schlong: Meyer, you idiot.

Sitter: Meyer is old.

Asher: He is ancient.

Dasher: (*approaches*) Talking behind my back?

Schlong: Behind Meyer's back.

Asher: He's too old.

Schlong: He's not in touch with the market.

Asher: He's bound to make mistakes.

Schlong: Costly mistakes.

Dasher: Meyer?

Asher: Who do you think?

Dasher: Meyer? But he's got no power? We've got the big accounts. The mutual funds, the money managers. He doesn't trade jellybeans anymore.

Schlong: Little mistakes add up. He can't hear.

Dasher: What?

Asher: He's deaf as a post.

Dasher: Meyer? I haven't talked to him in years. Why should I? Does he have anything to say?

Sitter: It wouldn't matter. He has no real power.

Asher: Let's fire him.

Sitter: We can't, he's a partner in the firm.

Dasher: What difference does that make?

Sitter: It means we can't fire him, without a darn good reason.

Asher: Let's find a reason, then fire him.

Schlong: Good thinking.

Asher: He is deaf.

Sitter: He wears a hearing aid. We can't fire him because of a handicap.

Schlong: He's incompetent.

Dasher: That should do it. Who wants to tell him?

Sitter: Tell him what?

Dasher: What else? That he is fired. Scram, beat it, vamos, get lost.

Schlong: He is the senior member of the partnership. He has seniority. He could have us fired.

Dasher: All the better that we should fire him first. Who is going to tell him?

Schlong: You tell him, Asher. It was your idea.

Asher: You called him incompetent.

Dasher: I'll do it. Come on. (*They cautiously approach Meyer's desk*)

Meyer: (*on phone*) Yes, Mr. Straight. You want a hundred Biometrics at the market? Yes, I can verify that. Yes, Mr. Bunker. I can do that. (*Looks around and sees them*) Hello, Dasher, Asher, Sitter, Schlong. Can I help you? (*Reaches into his pocket*)

Asher: (*to Sitter*) What's he doing?

Sitter: Turning down his hearing aid.

Dasher: I'm sorry to have to tell you this, Meyer, but we just had a little meeting.

Meyer: What you say?

Sitter: (*throwing up his hands*) Too late.

Dasher: You're fired!

Sitter: Too late.

Meyer: What you say?

Sitter: He's done this before. He can't hear a thing without a hearing aid and if he doesn't like what he's hearing he turns it off.

Dasher: You're fired!!!

Sitter: Really, it's too late. He didn't think you were friendly.

Dasher: I'm not.

Sitter: So you couldn't fire him. It's too late.

Dasher: I can't fire him?

Schlong: Not if he can't hear you.

Sitter: It wouldn't be fair, really.

Dasher: I want him out of here in 24 hours.

Asher: Let's vote.

Dasher: What the hell for?

Schlong: We are all partners. We should all have a vote.

Dasher: This is a brokerage house. Not a democracy. I want him out by noon tomorrow. I don't care how you do it. Noon tomorrow. (*exits*)

Asher: How can we fire him if he can't hear us? It isn't fair.

Sitter: He talks to some people.

Schlong: Just not to us.

Sitter: He talks to his customers.

All together: The telephone!

Asher: (*going to his desk and picking up the phone*) Helen, ring Mr. Meyer for me.

Poop: He's right over there.

Asher: I know he's there. Just do it, please. (*She rings his phone, Meyer picks it up*) This is Asher... The man is uncivil. He won't talk to his own partner.

Sitter: You are trying to fire him.

Schlong: He's on to us for sure.

Asher: How ancient is the old prick?

Schlong: He must be 80.

Asher: There must be a rule about that.

Sitter: You're allowed to die your desk. If you want.

Schlong: Like Miller.

Asher: Miller was only 35.

Sitter: Miller worked himself to death.

Asher: Unnecessarily.

Schlong: Miller was a fool. You really don't have to work so hard around here that you kill yourself.

Sitter: Meyer works harder than Miller any day. Meyer is a hard nut to crack.

Asher: A hard peach to can.

Schlong: A hard grain to sack.

Sitter: He won't die on the vine.

Asher: I've got it. We will have him committed.

Schlong: He is committed. He never takes a coffee break.

Asher: To a nursing home. We will have him declared incompetent.

Sitter: Impossible. What is your evidence? He lives by himself. Cooks his own meals. Rides to work on the subway. He has no vices except a movie on Saturday night. He fishes in Canada on his vacation and the rest of the time he is here.

Asher: Does he have relatives? Anyone who can testify against him?

Sitter: He has a sister. She hates him. She brings him his lunch everyday hoping that he is dead at his desk. She should be here by now.

Asher: Who besides the sister knows the real Malcolm Meyer?

Sitter: He has a son...They never talk to each other.

Asher: I put my father in a nursing home and he loves it. He hated living with me.

Schlong: I can see why.

Sitter: (*Enter Ethel Meyer*) There she is, the sister. Right on time.

Asher: Ms. Meyer, how good to see you again.

Ethel: Did I ever see you before?

Asher: It's about your brother.

Ethel: Is the old goat dead yet? Face down on his desk?

Asher: No.

Ethel: It's not that I haven't tried. Forty years of pastrami sandwiches and Hershey bars and his ticker is as sound as a clock. I am a physical wreck and he goes on working. The old goat. But if he does die? Who the devil cares? The stock market won't remember. Who will shed a tear for him? I won't. I have needed his money for years now. Now I am half dead myself. Still it would be nice to finally see the end of this thing. Pastrami isn't cheap these days. There he is at his desk. Not yet dead. The old duffer. What do you want from me?

Sitter: We've been told he must go before tomorrow noon.

Ethel: He won't go. Not unless he's dead or hauled away.

Schlong: We are thinking about hauled away.

Asher: Removed.

Schlong: Committed.

Asher: A nice shady place in the country.

Ethel: He won't go. I tried that 10 years ago. He's too smart.

Sitter: He mumbles. He is senile.

Ethel: He is senile all right, but he is senile shrewd. He's a clever vegetable. He won't sign forms. He will answer questions. He turns down his hearing aid or at least he pretends to.

Sitter: We know about that.

Ethel: He very seldom slips up.

Asher: All we need is one slip-up and we have him.

Ethel: He says some strange things.

Schlong: Like what?

Ethel: Ten years ago, out of the blue, he said "Buy IBM." Right out of the blue. I didn't know what to make of it.

Sitter: What did you do?

Ethel: I went shopping. Yes, I went shopping.

Asher: (*on phone to Poop*) Helen, I want a conference call with Meyer. Hook me up to his next customer.

Poop: Anyone in particular you want to spy on?

Asher: I don't care who. Just hook me on. (*to the others*) If we can't talk to him, we can listen. (*Phone rings*)

Poop: Yes, Mr. Meyer is in. (*Signals Asher. Meyer picks up*)

Asher: Here we go.

Schlong: What's he saying? Come on, we're part of this.

Asher: Shhhh. Hold on. (*Listens. Meyer hangs up*) Thank you.

Schlong: Come on, Asher. What did he say?

Asher: Buy Grambling, sell Ma Bell.

Schlong: What's Grambling?

Ethel: What's IBM?

Sitter: You mean sell Grambling, buy Ma Bell.

Asher: I swear. He said buy Grambling, sell Ma Bell.

Sitter: That's opposite to our market directory, contrary to our own research department.

Schlong: It's not what I told Central Bank and Trust.

Asher: I told you, he is senile. (*to Ethel*) You're his sister. You can have him committed if he is senile.

Ethel: He won't go to New Jersey. I have tried that.

Asher: We don't care where he goes. We just need your word that his mind is unsound, that he is unfit, and we can have him shipped off.

Ethel: My word and the signature of a psychiatrist.

Schlong: A psychiatrist?

Asher: A technicality. You will sign off if we get the evidence?

Ethel: If you would get rid of the old goat, I would drive him to New Jersey myself, but he won't go.

Asher: He'll go. (*Ethel goes toward Meyer*) What are you doing?

Ethel: The pastrami.

Asher: Leave that to us. Leave everything to us. Goodbye, Madam. (*Escorts Ethel, turns to Sitter and Schlong*). I should have said, leave everything to you two.

Sitter and Schlong: Us?

Asher: Noon tomorrow. I am going to lunch. (*Exits*)

Schlong: He can't do that. He can't leave the dirty work for us.

Sitter: He has seniority. Dartmouth class of '78.

Schlong: I'm Dartmouth class of '78.

Sitter: So am I. So is Dasher. But Asher took his diploma before us.

Schlong: He has ten minutes of seniority. Big deal. And I have two minutes of seniority over you. You call the psychiatrist.

Sitter: I don't know any.

Schlong: Dr. Beal is on our payroll. Call him.

Sitter: I thought he was for secretaries and wives.

Schlong: He's there for us too, if we ever need him.

Sitter: Our type doesn't go to psychiatrists, not willingly.

Schlong: I'd rather shoot myself. So just call him.

Sitter: (*Looks up number and dials*) Dr. Beal? Arnold Sitter here. Could you come to a thousand one Park Ave.? You are at a thousand one Park Ave.? Could you come up to the eighth floor? You are on the eighth floor. Could you come down the hall? Your office adjoins ours? You haven't been watching us have you? Could you come in here for a minute? I'm the one sitting under the Cancun travel poster. No, it's not for me. Okay I will see you in a minute. That was quick.

Schlong: Well?

Sitter: His office is right here. Just next door.

Schlong: He isn't spying on us, is he?

Sitter: I don't think so.

Schlong: He'd better not. We can fire him too.

Sitter: (*Beal enters*) That must be him, wave.

Schlong: (*Pulls his arm down*) He'll think we're crazy.

Beal: *(to Schlong)* You must be Mr. Sitter.

38

Schlong: He is Sitter. I'm Schlong.

Beal: It has been a Schlong time...Sorry.

Schlong: I've heard worse. We'll come to the point. We believe that one of our partners is no longer able to function in his duties.

Sitter: His behavior is erratic.

Schlong: His judgment is impaired.

Sitter: He is giving financial advice to the customers.

Schlong: We want to fire him.

Beal: I'm afraid I'm in the business of helping people with emotional problems find inner peace. All of us have rough points that need smoothing and there are crises that require intervention...

Schlong: We need to have him committed.

Beal: I have been of some help to several of the wives of members of your firm, a few secretaries, and one janitor. I've yet to treat any of the brokers.

Sitter: That is good news.

Beal: Maybe, maybe not. The fact is that all the partners are graduates of Dartmouth in the late 70s. It is strange, but true. Ivy League graduates of that vintage have been found not to possess true psyches. They simply exhibit patterns of behavior. Very little or no subconscious. I'm writing a paper on it.

Schlong: He's over there. Meyer is his name.

Beal: He looks old.

Sitter: Ancient.

Schlong: His sister will sign commitment papers. Just talk to him. It will become obvious.

Sitter: If he suspects anything he will shut his hearing aid off.

Beal: I must act ethically.

Schlong: He handles important clients. He is losing important business.

Beal: I cannot take any action without a thorough examination.

Sitter: Take your time.

Schlong: Just as long as his desk is clear by noon tomorrow.

Beal: Tomorrow?

Sitter: We have a deadline.

Beal: That would be impossible. The man must be tested.

Schlong: Can we fire you?

Beal: I suppose so. I guess I could accelerate the testing process. (*Starts towards Meyer*) What is his name?

Sitter: Meyer, Malcolm Meyer.

Beal: Thank you. (*Moves to Meyer's desk: they engage in a silent conversation*)

Schlong: Who wants the psyche after all? Just extra baggage if you ask me.

Sitter: He's coming back.

Schlong: (*to Beal*) Well...

Beal: I think he said buy Grambling, sell Ma Bell.

Sitter: And...

Beal: And then he shut off his hearing aid. (*Starts toward the door*)

Schlong: Where are you going?

Beal: Taking his advice. I hope it's not too late.

Schlong: (*following him halfway*) Come back here, Beal. You have to...(*off stage*) Beal, you are fired.

40

Sitter: (*looking at his computer*) Come here, Irving.

Schlong: (*turning away*) Psychiatrists are a dime a dozen.

Sitter (*excited*) Schlong, look here.

(Blackout.)

SCENE 2

Asher and Dasher sitting at desks reading travel brochures. Meyer busy with telephones as in the first scene. Schlong briefly stopping at Meyer's desk then coming to his own.

Asher: What did he say?

Schlong: Who?

Dasher: Meyer, you idiot.

Asher: What did he say?

Schlong: Nothing.

Asher: What did you ask him?

Schlong: Ask whom?

Dasher: Meyer, you dork.

Asher: You must have asked him something.

Schlong: He doesn't talk to me.

Dasher: He doesn't talk to anyone.

Asher: Except to his clients, who are making a pretty penny on this Ma Bell thing.

Dasher: Grambling was up four more points yesterday. Pretty good for a company that doesn't do any business. Doesn't make anything, doesn't sell anything, has no assets to speak of...

Asher: Except since Meyer found it, it has gone up...

Schlong: And up...

Dasher: And up...The bastard!

Schlong: Who?

Dasher: Meyer, you jerk.

(*Enter Sitter who passes by Meyer and stops briefly, then moves on to his desk*)

Asher, Dasher, Schlong together: What did he say?

Sitter: Nothing. He doesn't talk to me.

Asher: He won't talk to any of us.

Schlong: It's not as if we don't like him.

Asher: If he would only establish lines of communication.

Sitter: He is cutting himself off.

Dasher: I think we should shoot him.

Schlong: Here he comes.

(*Meyer approaches slowly, bent over. The others try not to notice*)

Meyer: (*to Sitter*) Now Ma Bell, that's a stock, eh Sitter?

Sitter: Huh...

Meyer: Look at the earnings. Look at the cash position, Look at the growth. It's like a gold mine.

Schlong: But you are selling Ma Bell. Been telling everyone to sell Ma Bell.

Meyer: Who me?

Dasher: Ya, you.

Meyer: It might go down a little, then right back up. You could sell Ma Bell if you like gambling.

All: GAMBLING!!!

Schlong: Not Grambling?

Meyer: What's Grambling?

Dasher: Grambling Inc., heavy metals, shipping...

Meyer: That dog. Who would buy that?

(*They rush to their phones*)

Asher: Dump Grambling!

Dasher: Mr. Wilcox, Meyer says Grambling is a dog.

Sitter: Treble, sell your Grambling. Yes a mistake. Buy Ma Bell.

Schlong: Helen, contact all my people. Those who bought Grambling. Tell them to get rid of it. Dump it all now. Tell them to buy Ma Bell.

Meyer: Our research boys love Ma Bell. All you have to do is read the reports. hose guys do a great job. (*Returns to his desk*)

Dasher: He has got to go. I want him out of here.

Sitter: He may be a genius.

Schlong: He keeps changing his mind.

Asher: He's inconsistent.

Schlong: A sure sign of senility.

Dasher: He is going to hurt us some day. Hurt us big time.

Sitter: Right now he's calling the shots.

Asher: He's been damn lucky, if you ask me.

Dasher: He could have burned us with this Grambling thing.

Schlong: It wasn't his fault. We just heard him wrong.

Asher: He doesn't speak clearly (*telephone*) Hello. (*to others*) It's Central Bank. Yes, Mr. Fargo. Yes, Mr. Fargo. The Grambling thing. Yes, of course. (to Fargo) Goodbye Mr. Fargo. (to others) It was Fargo at Central Bank. Grambling has dropped out of sight. Down 15 at the opening. The company is filing Chapter 11.

Schlong: We lost the account.

Asher: No, they got out at the top. They made 10 million, in and out. They wanted to congratulate our research department. They are going to recommend us to their subsidiaries.

All: Meyer!

(*Sitter gets up to tell Meyer*)

Dasher: Where are you going?

Sitter: To congratulate him.

Dasher: What the hell for? We made the recommendation.

Sitter: It was his idea.

Dasher: You heard him. He didn't know what he was doing. It was just an unfortunate mistake that we had the foresight to turn into a big winner. Come on, Sitter, we can't let our emotions get in the way of sound business management practices.

Sitter: He's just a tired old man. It might give him a lift, or at least a laugh.

Dasher: Can it, Arnold, come over here. We've got work to do. (*Sitter returns*) That's better. Okay, I'm going to get some coffee. Anybody? All right, I'll celebrate by myself. (*Exits*)

(*Meyer gets on the phone*)

Poop: Yes, Mr. Meyer. Yes, Mr. Meyer (*She rings Sitter*) Arnold, it's Mr. Meyer.

Sitter: (*picks up phone*) Yes... yes... yes... yes... yes.... Thank you, Mr. Meyer, Malcolm. Goodbye. Thank you.

Asher and Schlong: What is it?

Sitter: He thinks there's going to be a big depression. Says that he should know. He was around in '29. It smells the same to him.

Schlong: Smells?

Sitter: Something in the air. He says he can smell it.

Asher: Metaphorically?

Sitter: He says he can taste it in his mouth when he wakes up in the morning.

Schlong: Like cigar smoke?

Sitter: He wanted to warn us. He says I'm the only one he trusts. He likes me.

Asher: What if the old fart is right? What about the market? How does he know?

Sitter: He smells something.

Asher: He must have some information. Some data. Some guidance. Who is tipping him off?

Schlong: What if he is right? I'm going to call Futzmueller. Have them sell some of the cyclicals.

Sitter: He said we should buy stock.

Schlong and Asher: Buy?

Sitter: He's telling all of his people to buy them. Buy heavy.

Asher: Going into a recession?

Schlong: A depression?

Asher: He's lost it.

Sitter: He was right on Ma Bell.

Asher: He was only following the research department. We're talking about a depression. We're talking about the whole goddam economy. Down the tubes. And he wants to buy stock. He is nuts.

Sitter: He's been around a long time.

Asher: Dasher is right. Meyer has been around too long. He's a walking fruitcake. Speaking of which, I'm going to lunch. Coming Irving?

Schlong: Sure.

Asher: Come on, Arnold give it up. Whoever heard of buying into a recession?

Sitter: A depression.

Asher: I'm buying into a meatball sandwich myself. Coming?

Schlong: Arnold?

Sitter: I got to make a few calls.

Asher: Don't do anything stupid. (*They exit*)

Sitter: (*Looks over to Meyer, who waves at him, Sitter hesitates, then waves back. After thinking a moment picks up the phone*) Hello, may I speak to Mr. Curling. Mr. Curling, Arnold Sitter here. Do you have a minute? It could mean a lot of money.

(*Blackout*)

SCENE THREE

(Asher, Dasher, Schlong and Sitter are feverishly answering telephones. Everybody talks at once.)

Dasher: Yes, 200 shares of Tourcotte, at the market.

Asher: I'll do the best I can, Mr. Ambrose. It's just a question of catching it right now.

Sitter: It's up 3 1/2 since this morning. You might not be able to get a correction.

Schlong: Get a thousand Textron, and a thousand MoCo. Of course, we'll try to get it at 89. If it's a point higher? Sure, we'll do the best we can.

Dasher: Yes, Mr. Tree. I'm afraid last night's closing is out of the question. Mostar is up 4 points since the close. I really can't promise anything. A thousand shares at the market. Thank you, Mr. Tree.

Asher: It's up six points, Gary. I'll try to get UN. They are panicking. 100 million shares and it isn't even noon. I can't sit and talk now.

Sitter: No, Mr. Tarr. We haven't seen anything like it. The blue chips are flying. We're telling everybody that if they hesitate now they looking at much higher prices. A thousand IBM. Of course, you can have margin.

Schlong: Mom, I just wouldn't wait if I were you. This is the chance of a decade to get in on a real bull market.

Dasher: Yes, Mr. Short....Yes, Mr. Sun....Why, yes, Mr. Wright.

Asher: Very good.... will do ... very good... will do.

Sitter: We'll do our best... sure... yes, buy, at the market...

Schlong: Thank you, Mr. Strong... hold on, Mr. Grant...

(Bell rings. They all shout, throw papers into the air, hug each other)

Dasher: What a day!!

Asher: Record volume... 200 billion shares... 200 billion shares.

Sitter: We're rich... if we weren't rich already. Even the customers are rich.

Schlong: I can't believe it... I just can't believe it.

Sitter: And just think, Meyer said it would happen.

Dasher: Meyer?

Sitter: He told us to buy. He got us in at the bottom. I told you he was a genius.

Dasher: Meyer told you to buy? Is that right, Asher?

Asher: Just before the market turn.

Schlong: I think we should congratulate him.

Dasher: Anybody who makes me rich is a friend of mine.

Sitter: You wanted to shoot him yesterday.

Dasher: Me? Did I say that? If I did, I was kidding. Come on. (*Goes to Meyer's desk*) Put her there, hip, hip,

All: Hooray, speech, speech!!

Meyer: My... my... my...... I just want to say, I want to say...

Asher: How did you do it, old man?

Meyer: It smelled like shoe polish. I remember the shoe polish, 1929. I went to get my shoes polished. They started jumping... everybody was screaming... grown men. I remember one old man running out of a can with his pants down, just screaming his fool head off. Someone had shot himself in the can next to him. Some people today don't think they were killing themselves. Just over money. I saw it all. Money was important then.

Asher: Still is...

Meyer: It was shoe polish on Black Tuesday. They called it Black Tuesday. It smelled everywhere of shoe polish and guns and grown men jumping. People running everywhere. Heart attacks, there were a lot of them. People running with their pants down yelling at the top of their lungs... buy...buy. buy..

Schlong: You mean sell.

Meyer: It was just like today. People all excited. Telephones ringing. The beginning of the Great Depression. Buy..buy...buy...

Asher: In '29 they were all selling. The stock market crash. They were all yelling sell, not buy.

Meyer: Sell? Was it sell? Maybe it was, sell. I remember the shoe polish.

(Blackout).

SCENE FOUR

(*The office is empty except for Meyer slumped over his desk. Enter Earl, the janitor, sweeping up. He stops at Meyer's desk, shakes him*)

Earl: Mr. Meyer, sir. Lord, he is dead. Help. Mr. Meyer please wake up. (*Meyer stirs*) Thank God, you are alive. I thought you were dead. Lord, you know how I hate dead people. I am glad you are alive. Are you okay, Mr. Meyer?

Meyer: Am I dead?

Earl: Oh, no, Mr. Meyer. You look alive to me, sir.

Meyer: Am I working?

Earl: You were working slow, Mr. Meyer. Working slow.

Meyer: Is that you, Earl?

EarL; Yes, sir, Mr. Meyer. It's me, Earl.

Meyer: I'll be finished in a minute. Have to be ready for tomorrow. People expect more out of me now that the depression is back. They need to make money. They don't just want it. They need it.

Earl: I wouldn't know about money, Mr. Meyer. I got no use for money. I got my paycheck. That's all I care about. The Missus takes care of everything. I haven't seen money since I was unemployed. No, sir. I waited in line for it, then I used to buy liquor. Unemployment is no good, Mr. Meyer. You see too much money when you're not working. It's not good for a man.

Meyer: You should be buying stock, Earl. Depression is a good time to buy companies. Somebody bought Southern Oil today. One man could buy an entire company. Can't do that when times are good. What about CSH? CSH is a plum, a real plum.

Earl: I don't care much for fruit, Mr. Meyer. Rice and bourbon, not too much fruit. Maybe an apple, once a month, for a change.

Meyer: That's not much to sustain a man.

Earl: My wife eats what I eat, Mr. Meyer. Rice and bourbon. TV and the Bible.

Meyer: A life full of contradictions.

Earl: And solutions. I couldn't live on rice and TV alone. The Bible is my salvation.

Meyer: We tread a far different road, Earl.

Earl: Oh no, sir. I have watched you. I've watched you on and off for 30 years, and I suppose you weren't any different before I came. You're not like these young ones.

Meyer: Asher, Dasher...

Earl:... Sitter, Schlong. They are all the same to me. No, you are different. You are a religious man.

Meyer: No.

Earl: Yes, sir. You practice your religion right here. Your congregation is the telephone wire. This is your church and here is your pulpit.

Meyer: That's a computer terminal, Earl.

Earl: It's just the way I see it, Mr. Meyer. I don't speak for no one else but me.

Meyer: My customers just want to make money.

Earl: We all have our own church. Your people believe in money, we believe in everlasting life. It's all the same.

Meyer: What if I switch to everlasting life?

Earl: Then you would be more like us.

Meyer: That wouldn't be so bad.

Earl: Some folks it don't fit.

Meyer: 50 years in stocks and bonds. Maybe I'm in a rut.

Earl: Getting saved is easy. It don't take no college degree.

Meyer: That would let me out.

Earl: It don't matter which way. Would you believe that I am an ordained minister myself? Come pray with me, brother. (*Kneels down*)

Meyer: I don't think I'm ready.

Earl: From the looks of you, I wouldn't diddle around too much longer. Come on, kneel with me.

Meyer: (*Kneels*) This will be a first.

Earl: Oh, Lord, look down upon us sinners, especially this doddery one by my side. Mr. Meyer, here is a sinner. A sinner like the rest of us. But by the looks he hasn't too many sins of the flesh. I would say his sins are more of a financial order. Picking the pockets of poor folks to feed the fat cats. Playing off the government to the people and the people to big business. Raking down the coals that fire the boilers of the banks and the Fortune 500. Playing harp at the financial roundtables and organ for the Trilateral Commission.

Meyer: I'm just a stockbroker, Earl.

Earl: The Lord don't mind a bit of exaggeration. In short, Mr. Meyer is a man who has sucked at the skin of society so that the pulp and seeds have popped into the mouths of the wealthy few. Now, oh Lord, this sinner comes to you willing to give up all that is manipulative and shrewd so as to walk alone with you. To eat a simple crust, with maybe a sip of bourbon now and then. To praise a man and not his hollow instruments of trade and greed. To give up that ten to four floating crap game that man calls Wall Street for the sake of an everlasting world beyond. He is asking this knowing that no new road is clear of obstacles, that he has but a short period on earth to clean up his act. He asks all this in your name, oh Lord, amen. Say amen.

Meyer: Amen.

Earl: That's it.

Meyer: I'm saved?

Earl: Do you accept Jesus Christ as your personal savior?

Meyer: Yes, I guess.

Earl: Then you are saved.

(*Blackout.*)

SCENE FIVE

(*Asher, Dasher, Sitter, Schlong sitting reading papers and travel brochures. Meyer taking calls. As scene develops Meyer pauses to drape a huge Jesus Saves sign over his desk.*)

Asher: I'm sick of the Bahamas.

Dasher: You mean you are sick of the sun? The endless nights of rum and women, tropical breezes and hot sand beaches?

Asher: No, just the Bahamas.

Schlong: There is always St. Bart's.

Sitter: Crete is nice. If you'd like a change.

Schlong: Samoa. What about American Samoa?

Asher: You have to cross the dateline. I hate crossing the dateline. It ruins my day.

Sitter: (*telephone*) Yes, Mr. Meyer, good morning to you too. (*to others*) It's Meyer. Yes... yes... yes... I'll ask around... I'll have to give it some thought... thank you, anyway... goodbye.

Schlong: What is it?

Dasher: What is that idiot up to now?

Sitter: He wants me to sell everything. He's telling all his people to dump all their stocks and bonds.

Dasher: He's a dope. We're in the biggest bull market of the decade.

Schlong: He's been right before.

Dasher: A lucky mistake.

Sitter: He got us in the bottom.

Asher: He thinks the market is topping out?

Sitter: He didn't say that. He said God did not like stocks and bonds.

All: God?

Asher: God doesn't like stocks and bonds?

Sitter: That's what he said.

Dasher: He's saying God is un-American?

Sitter: I can just say what he told me.

Schlong: Did he say that God didn't like stocks and bonds in the short term or over the long haul?

Sitter: He didn't go into details.

Asher: Did he say what God did like? Options, money market funds, futures?

Sitter: He mentioned the United Way.

Schlong: The United Way.

Dasher: (*looking madly through the paper*) Must be on the American Exchange.

Sitter: I think it's a charity.

Asher: He's giving money away?

Sitter: His own money?

Asher: Must be a tax shelter.

Sitter: ..and he is strongly recommending that his customers give up all theirworldly possessions.

All: The customers?

Sitter: I can only tell you what he told me. He suggests that we do the same. He thinks the world would be a better place.

Dasher: He's gone too far this time. This is a brokerage house, not the Salvation Army. This man is old, senile, and he is dangerous. I want him out of here by tomorrow morning, Lock, stock, and barrel. (*Picks up telephone*) Helen, hold my calls.

Poop: It's Northeast Bank, Mr. Dasher. They want to know what to do about Limited Electronics.

Dasher: (*to others*) I want him out, his papers burned and his desk put out on the street. We can't have his thoughts contaminating our office routine. I'm getting some coffee,

Poop: What should I tell the bank, Mr. Dasher?

Dasher: Tell them to sell the shit out of everything they've got. (*Exits*)

Asher: I guess I could use some coffee.

Sitter and Schlong: Ya. (*Asher exits*)

Schlong: Coffee doesn't sound bad. (*Rises*) Want any?

Sitter: No, thanks. (*Sitter looks to Meyer who waves and winks and points to the telephone. Sitter waves back. Picks up the telephone*) Helen, would you give a ring to my best accounts. Tell them to lighten up all over. No, tell them to sell everything.

Poop: Everything?

Sitter: Yes, everything. (*Asher enters as Sitter leaves*) Coffee. (*Exits*)

Asher: Forgot my date book (*After Sitter leaves, picks up phone*) Helen, could you get Finkelstein on the phone… I want to sell all the stocks he can get his hands on. Same for Central Bank. Shoot, call everybody.

Poop: Sell?

Asher: Yes, sell, sell everything. (*Schlong enters*) Coffee. (*Exits*)

Schlong: Forgot my datebook. (*Picks up phone*) Helen…

Poop: Sell everything?

Schlong: How did you know? Call everybody, sell everything.

Poop: What should they do with the money?

Schlong: Hey, don't ask me. Give it to charity. No, of course not, I'm joking. Thank you, Helen. (*Exits bumping into Anson Meyer on the way out*) Excuse me.

Anson: (*going to Meyer's desk and standing there on the scene for a moment*) Hi, Dad.

Meyer: Anson, it's you. I thought it was one of those Dartmouth pricks. My eyesight isn't so good anymore. You certainly don't look like an Ivy Leaguer.

Anson: You went to Princeton.

Meyer: That was 50 years ago. Besides we didn't learn to be a prick in those days.

Anson: You didn't learn anything in those days. Except how to play cards and wear a raccoon coat.

Meyer: What do you want?

Anson: I came for a visit.

Meyer: It's not a good time for visiting; the market is like a yo-yo.

Anson: Then you could miss one bounce for your only son. It will come right back to you, won't it?

Meyer: Not this time, Son. I'm getting out and staying out. (*pause*) Nothing to say? Did you want me to quit?

Anson: 20 years ago.

Meyer: I've been saved.

Anson: Is that better than being preserved?

Meyer: I'm giving up my worldly possessions. I can't wait until those Dartmouth pricks find out. They think I'm selling to beat the Bears. I'm selling to beat the band. That's what I'm doing. They think I've lost it, but they are afraid I may be right.

Anson: They follow your lead?

Meyer: Because I am right. They would be lost without me. Another great reason for getting out now.

Anson: You'll make a fortune.

Meyer: My accounts will be saved. I don't have any real accounts. A few old ladies in Florida. Most everybody else is dead. Everybody is either retired or dead or they went to Dartmouth.

Anson: And you come to work, each and every day. What a life. Just for the money?

Meyer: It's a game. Who cares about the money? I'm giving the money away. That should kill your aunt. The old vulture. The United Way, Son.

Anson: Sounds like a stock or something.

Meyer: I am selling my seat on the exchange. Unless you want it, Son.

Anson: You know me, Dad.

Meyer: The seat has been in the family for five generations.

Anson: You said it, Dad, it's a game.

Meyer: And you don't play games? Antiwar this, ban the bomb that. Those aren't games? What does it get you? Heck, maybe I'll give you the seat. It's worth a quarter of a million. What you couldn't do with a quarter of a million. You could buy Central America. Idealism takes money, too. Or haven't you found that out yet? Money helps to grease the wheels of all causes.

Anson: Money isn't the problem.

Meyer: It is when you're old.

Anson: My generation is not going to live to get old.

Meyer: Want to bet?

Anson: We'll all go together in one atomic cloud.

Meyer: Whoopee. We're all going to die in a ball of fire. (*pause*) How come you don't have a sense of humor?

Anson: (*turning to go*) I'm still young.

Meyer: Well, it was nice to see you. Maybe, you will come back and see me again in a few years.

Anson: Right.

Meyer: You might see a changed man.

Anson: Right. (*Exits. Sitter enters and approaches Meyer's desk*)

Sitter: Hey, the Dow is down 100 points. American Steel is shutting its Burlingame plant. I think it's a real breakpoint, a classic head and shoulders. Rollercoasterville. (*Meyer holds head and sinks in his chair*) What's wrong, Mr. Meyer?

Meyer: Just a little dizzy, that's all.

Sitter: Don't worry, we are out. So what if the market takes a beating? It's not the end of the world.

Meyer: Right, it's not the end of the world. (*Blackout*)

SCENE SIX

(Earl is at Meyer's desk working carefully with his screwdriver dismantling Meyer's computer. Enter Meyer who crosses and observes.)

Earl: Oh, Mr. Meyer, it's you.

Meyer: Taking me apart, eh, Earl?

Earl: I hear they're putting in a video game.

Meyer: Nothing would surprise me. I shall leave without a shadow. 50 years at one desk. I was sitting here before they were born.

Earl: Time left to enjoy life. Have a little fun. That's the best thing about being saved, if you ask me.

Meyer: What's that?

Earl: More time for having fun. You can save the hard stuff for the hereafter.

Meyer: The hard stuff?

Earl: You've seen them jumping for joy in church. Jumping right into the air. Screaming, I've been saved, I've been saved. You ever ask saved from what?

Meyer: The hard stuff?

Earl: You bet your ass.

Meyer: I'm not sure I'm ready for that.

Earl: That's the best part. And just think you can start right now.

Meyer: Could you help me with this package?

Earl: I wish I could start right now. It helps if you've got a little cash put away. *(getting up)*

Meyer: It's over by the elevator door. *(They go offstage)*

Earl: *(re-entering followed by Meyer)* That's quite a package. *(Pushes on stage a huge gift box on hand car)* This is your retirement party. You're

58

supposed to get the gifts.

Meyer: It's just a going away thing. Right over here if you don't mind. Careful!

Earl: (*lifting it onto the desk*) This is one heavy package. (*Meyer exits*)
Frankly, I don't see why you want to give them anything. They haven't been...
Mr. Meyer?

Meyer: (*re-enters carrying another box*) Well, that should do it. (*Puts second
box on top of the first, withdraws an envelope*) Earl, this is for you.

Earl: (*taking envelope*) Really, Mr. Meyer. You shouldn't have. (*Begins to
open*)

Meyer: No, not now. After the party.

Earl: I don't know what to say.

Meyer: Don't thank me yet. Goodnight, Earl. See you tomorrow.

Earl: Goodnight, Mr. Meyer. Remember, don't forget about the fun part.

Meyer: I won't. (*Exits slowly*)

(*Earl pockets envelope, returns to work.*)

(*Blackout*)

SCENE SEVEN

(*Some party decorations set up. Asher, Dasher, Sitter and Schlong wearing
party hats*)

Dasher: No speeches. Three cheers and I want him out of here. I have work
to do. Speeches are out. This is a brokerage house not a charity ball.

Sitter: He's been here for 50 years.

Dasher: Half the time he's been running down the business.

Asher: He's lost all the good accounts.

Schlong: His clients died.

Asher: A lost account is a lost account.

Dasher: He should have been nicer to the heirs.

Sitter: He didn't relate to the new generation. Youth is so impatient.

Schlong: They want to lose an inheritance overnight.

Sitter: Here he comes.

Schlong: For he's a jolly good fellow…

Asher: Not yet. It's too soon for that.

Schlong: Sorry.

Sitter: (*to Meyer*) Afternoon. How was lunch?

Meyer: Can't listen to your hunch right now. Got some last-minute paperwork. Today's my last day, you know.

Schlong: Poor devil. He thinks we don't know.

Asher: He can't hear a thing.

Sitter: What's he going to do with himself?

Dasher: He's got money up the wing wang.

Sitter: He has got no one. His relatives won't have him.

Dasher: What's the difference? This is not an old age home.

Sitter: It's just sad.

Schlong: He's got religion.

Dasher: What the devil do you care?

Asher: Let's get it over with now. (*Moves towards Meyer's desk*)

Schlong: The market is still open.

Dasher: To hell with the market. Let's do it.

All: For he's a jolly good fellow, for he's a jolly good fellow, for he's a jolly good fellow which nobody can deny. (Meyer takes no notice)

Sitter: (handing him a present) Just a little something from us to you.

(Meyer takes it slowly without expression)

Sitter: I think it's real gold... coated. It's water resistant.

Asher: And a real buy at $21.95. (popping the champagne cork) Champagne? Champagne? (Meyer puts on the watch)

Sitter: Speech! Speech!

All except Dasher: Speech! Speech on the table! (They lift him onto the table next to the enormous box) Speech! Speech!

Meyer: This has been a long time... 50 years... a long time coming.

Dasher: I hope this is short.

Meyer: Miller? Are you out there? Miller?

Schlong: Miller's been dead for 15 years.

Meyer: Miller, are you out there?

Dasher: Miller's dead.

Meyer: You understood it, didn't you, Miller? You aren't like these young ones. The market was a science to you, wasn't it, Miller? They think it's a dart board now. A fat living for preppy dartboard artists. That's what it is? The market hasn't changed. We have changed haven't we, Miller? We have made good in our lives. We haven't changed the world... we haven't changed a goddam thing. People die playing this game. People die and never go to heaven. Some people never find God.

Asher: He's gonzo.

Schlong: He's lost it.

Meyer: Don't you see, Miller, we've wasted it all. Every day we came here. The subway, the walk, the elevator, the desk. We never had computers in those days, did we Miller?

Asher: This is nostalgia gone sour.

Dasher: Throttle him will you.

Poop: Who is Miller?

Sitter: Shush.

Meyer: Give me my piece. Give me my piece, you preppy bastards. Fifty years at this goddam desk. This race track. We gave the people the Great Depression. We gave them bread lines, didn't we, Miller? We gave them Roosevelt. We gave them the Vietnam War and Iraq. We set the price of gas. You and me, Miller.

Schlong: Miller was a baby then.

Meyer: We killed them all and sent home the bodies. We made the bullets. We made the bombs. We made the big bomb. We scared the shit out of the whole world. And we made money at it. We made money, and we didn't care. The market went up. We made money. The market went down. We made more money. It didn't matter, not in this game.

Sitter: Champagne?

Meyer: (*Takes it*) Thank you. (*Sips*) So who was saved...Miller? Did we save you?

Sitter: Miller is dead.

Meyer: Miller wasn't saved. Miller wasn't saved. Who shall save the world? Who shall stop this horrible game? Who shall stop the death? Who shall stop the bombs?

Dasher: I want this stopped. Asher, do something.

Meyer: Who shall stop the bombs? You Asher? You Sitter? You Schlong? You Dasher?

Dasher: This is a brokerage house, not the Pentagon.

Meyer: I want an answer. I want an answer.

Dasher: Get down, you senile old bastard. Your day is over. I've had it with you!

Meyer: Not yet, you haven't. Not just yet. (*Pulls open the package revealing what appears to be a bomb with detonator*) Nobody leaves this room. I've got dynamite in here. Don't think I don't. (*They scramble behind their desks, Dasher runs to the exit*) Don't move or I'll blow the hell out of this building. (*Dasher stops*) Okay Sitter, I'll have a little sip of that champagne if you don't mind. (*getting down off the desk*)

Dasher: Well, Sitter, do what he says. (*Sitter moves nervously with bottle*) Go on, you wienie, go!

Sitter: Why don't you go, Dasher if you are so brave?

Meyer: I want you, Arnold. I don't trust those other bastards.(*Sitter crosses. Meyer and Arnold take the champagne and duck behind Meyer's desk taking the detonator with them*)

Dasher: Doesn't trust us? Doesn't trust us? He sitting behind the bomb, he doesn't trust us?

Meyer: Helen, come here, and bring the rest of the champagne.

Poop: (*Gathers champagne and joins Meyer. Sticks tongue out at the others*)

Schlong: (*Grabs phone*) I'm calling the cops.

Dasher: (*grabbing phone*) Don't be a fool. That's what he wants. To ruin us. cops, reporters. People will think we run a psychiatric ward here. We have to handle this ourselves. Schlong, you call his sister, his son, that doctor, what's his name?

Asher: Beal.

Dasher: Beal. I want them here right away.

Schlong: We're going to talk him down?

Dasher: We are going to talk him down then blow his brains out.

Asher: Why Dr. Beal?

Dasher: We need a witness to show that he was mad. We wouldn't want to shoot a partner unless he was a mad dog, would we?

Schlong: Of course not.

Dasher: Asher, you have heart problems.

Asher: I am fine.

Dasher: Take it from me, you have heart problems. I want you to get the gun.

Asher: I don't know anything about guns. Where would I get a gun?

Dasher: There are four million handguns in the city. Just find one. Pay cash.

Asher: I feel sick.

Dasher: That's my boy. (*standing up*) Meyer, Asher is having chest pains. He's got to get some fresh air.

Meyer: Does he promise to stop building bombs?

Dasher: The man is sick.

Meyer: Does he promise?

Dasher: He promises to come back after he feels better to let you blow him up.

Meyer: That's not good enough.

Dasher: Yeah, he promises.

Meyer: I want to hear it from him.

Asher: I promise.

Meyer: Okay, he can go but he must come back.

Dasher: (*to Asher*) Go. And don't get some BB gun. I want his brains out.

Asher: I'll be right back. (*Begins to rise*)

Dasher: Act sick, you dummy.

Asher: (*Stumbles to exit*)

Schlong: (*to Dasher*) Okay, they're on their way. (*Puts the phone down*)Beal's just down the hall.

Dasher: Then where is he? (*Beal has entered from behind*)

Schlong: Right behind you.

Dasher: Beal, I'm glad you're here. Get down.

Beal: What's the problem?

Dasher: Meyer's gone mad. He has a bomb.

Deal: He has an unusual mind. His market advice has always been helpful.

Dasher: A bomb! TNT! Dynamite! Kaboom!

Beal: What do you want me to do?

Dasher: Talk him down.

Beal: What about police? A psychiatrist?

Dasher: What do we pay you a year, Beal?

Beal: $70,000. I'll talk to him. Mr. Meyer, may I have a word with you?

Meyer: Dr. Beal, come right over. Bring a glass.

Dasher: What did he say?

Beal: Bring a glass.

Dasher: Do it. I told you he was a loony.

Meyer: A champagne glass. Did you know this is my going away party?

Dasher: (*to Beal*) Go, do what he says.

Beal: Here I come.

Schlong: I have his sister here.

Dasher: How did she get here so fast?

Schlong: She's very greedy for one thing. She took the A train.

(*Enter Ethel. We hear some talk and laughter from Meyer, Beal, Poop and Sitter from behind the desk*)

Ethel: Is he dead yet?

Schlong: He's trying to kill us.

Ethel: Oh, yes, he used to hit me with snowballs. Icy ones.

Dasher: He wants to blow up the building.

Ethel: Oh, my, it's getting worse. Well, as long as he's getting his. What's the difference? It's been a long tiring wait.

Dasher: You're in the building he's trying to blow up.

Ethel: The snotty-nosed bastard. To think he is two years younger than I am. Malcolm, what are you up to?

Meyer: World peace. Have some champagne.

Ethel: (*to Dasher*) One of his tricks. Malcolm, remember when you made me a snow fort? It took you three days after school. Then you had me go in. And you threw those icy balls at me and it caved in on my head. Are you doing the same thing now?

Meyer: Yes!

Ethel: Remember how I cried and ran into the house and told Mommy that you tricked me and she gave you a spanking and sent you to your room without dinner and you cried until she let you come out, but made you promise never to build snow forts that caved in and make me go into them and made you apologize to me and to love me and share all your toys and give me bubble gum when you had some and not cheat in marbles while we waited for the school bus and share your money which you never did so now I am stuck in the Bronx with a bad hip and can't go to Palm Beach because my cost-of-living allowance is only 7%. Are you pulling that same number on me again by threatening to blow up the building with me and everyone else in it in the abstract name of world peace? (*pause*) Answer me, old brother of mine.

Meyer: Yes!

Ethel: So?

Meyer: So go home. (*Dasher makes a break for it*) Not you, Dasher. (*Dasher stops short and goes back*)

Ethel: Thank you, Malcolm. (*to Dasher*) You have to know how to talk to him. (*Exits*)

Schlong: (*to Dasher*) His son is here.

Dasher: Send him in.

Anson: (*Enters*) What's wrong? Someone called.

Dasher: Your father has flipped. He wants to blow us up. Something about world peace.

Schlong: None of us can leave.

Anson: Dad, is that you?

Meyer: Anson, what are you doing here?

Anson: Is it true what they say?

Meyer: (*obviously tipsy*) Everything is false, and true, at the same time. Grab a glass son.

Anson: Do you have a bomb?

Meyer: Do I have a bomb? Arnold, do I have a bomb?

Sitter: (*also drunk*) Does he have a bomb?

Meyer: Dr. Beal, do I have a bomb?

Beal: Your father is a very interesting man.

Dasher: Ask him about bombing for peace.

Anson: Dad, why you doing this?

Meyer: I want people to stop. I want people to look. I want people to listen. I am a railroad crossing sign.

Anson: Does this have anything to do with nuclear disarmament?

Meyer: I want to help you.

Anson: If you wanted to help me, you would have done something a long time ago. You were always too tired or too busy. Don't bother your father, he's too tired, he's too busy. Why were you always so old? Too old to play baseball, or too tired, or too busy. What did you ever give me? World peace is my thing. Why do you want it? I make a living doing what I do. I don't need any 80-year-old dilettantes marching in my parade.

Meyer: I see you on TV. I am proud of you, son, and want to help you. I watched it all happen. I was part of it. I want it to stop.

Anson: I don't want your help. Not this way. Will you come out?

Meyer: Want some champagne? There are three more bottles. Do you want my seat on the exchange? It's not too late.

Anson: No, I don't want the seat. Please come out.

Meyer: Don't you understand? I have nothing to believe in.

Anson: That is not my fault. (*to Dasher*) There's nothing more I can do. Goodbye, Dad. (*Exits. Asher re-enters carrying a package. Meyer gets up to look*)

Meyer: Son! Oh, it's you, Asher. Feeling better are you?

Sitter: (*pulling Meyer back down*) Maybe you better lay off the champagne.

Asher: (*to Dasher and Schlong*) I got it.

Dasher: What is it?

Schlong: That's no handgun.

Asher: It's the best I could get. Army surplus.

Dasher: (*unwrapping submachine gun*) Good God!

Asher: It's an Israeli. You put the bullets in here. The guy said it was quiet. Phuttt, Phuttt, Phutt. That's the sound.

Dasher: What guy?

Asher: A friend of someone in maintenance. I got a good deal. I think it's hot.

Dasher: Did you tell them we were starting a war?

Asher: You said a gun, I got a gun. He gave me a receipt.

Dasher: It will do. He said he put the bullets in here, did he? Okay, let's give it a go.

Asher: (*pulling gun down*) What about Sitter, Dr. Beal, Helen?

Dasher: You spoiled my shot.

Schlong: Call the others back.

Asher: I'll do it. Dr. Beal, Helen, could we have a word with you? (*to Dasher*) Put down the gun. They can see it.

Beal: Just a second, hold my glass. (*Hands glass to Sitter and with Helen crosses the room to the other side*)

Poop: Be right back, you sweet old man.

Beal: (*to Helen*) That is first-rate champagne.

Asher: What did he say?

Beal: We were talking about the crash of '29.

Poop: Did you know it was all started with shoe polish?

Dasher: He is crazy.

Beal: He's a bit dotty.

Poop: But sweet.

Beal: I feel a bit dotty myself.

Dasher: Is he going to blow us up?

Beal: I forgot to ask. Hold on a second. (*Walks back and has a few silent words with Meyer*) He says yes, unless you sell your defense stocks.

Asher: Which ones?

Beal: Be right back. (*Goes and returns*) American Nuclear, Assorted Technologies, and Poomingdale's.

Dasher: Bloomingdale's?

Beal: It sounded like Poomingdale's. He has had a bit of champagne.

Asher: They make warheads. (*Beal staggers towards the exit*)

Dasher: Where are you going?

Beal: To sell American Nuclear, Assorted Technologies, Poomingdale's, and throw up. Will you join me in this, Poop?

Poop: Don't mind if I do. (*They exit together*)

Dasher: *(raising gun)* Now are you satisfied?

Schlong: We have to get Arnold out. Arnold. Arnold. Could we have a word with you?

Sitter: (*to Meyer*) Just a minute. I'll be right back, Malcolm. (*Crosses and sees gun*) What's that?

Asher: Shhh, be quiet.

Sitter: No, you can't.

Dasher: He wants to blow us up, Arnold. This is self-defense. Meyer is crazy. He is going to blow us up if we don't stop him. If ever a word gets out why he wanted to blow us up, we're out of business gentlemen, we're finished. We might as well sell hot dogs in Woodmere.

Sitter: He's just a confused old man.

Dasher: My ass. He is a danger to himself and others. He is dangerous to himself and others and we need him dead.

Sitter: I've been talking to him. He's not really serious.

Dasher: Then ask him. Ask him if he is serious or not.

Sitter: (*yelling across barricades*) Malcolm, are you really going to blow us upif we don't support world peace?

Dasher: Notice he can hear things when he wants to. Meyer, this is a sovereign brokerage concern.

Sitter: Let me handle this. Is that your final demand?

Meyer: Sell Assorted Technologies.

Sitter: There, he has reduced his demands.

Dasher: Meyer, are you trying to blackmail us?

Sitter: Is this something we can talk about, Malcolm? Is this something you want to die for?

Meyer: What? Goddam hearing aid. (*standing up*)

Sitter: Can you hear me? Is this something you're willing to die for?

Meyer: (*Stands up, Dasher takes aim*)

Sitter: Malcolm!

Meyer: I think I'm going to be sick. (*Dasher shoots, Malcolm falls*)

Dasher: (*dropping the gun, they run toward Meyer*) Get the bomb! Get the goddam bomb.

Sitter: My God. Call an ambulance. My God.

Dasher: Help me open this thing. Asher, Schlong, Sitter. Leave him. This may go off any minute.

Schlong: (*Beal and Poop re-enter*) Dr. Beal, he's been shot. Get an ambulance, quick (*Poop exits*)

Sitter: (*holding up Meyer with Beal*) He wants Earl.

Beal: Earl who?

Sitter: Earl the janitor. Schlong, get Earl.

Schlong: Where?

Sitter: Just get him.

Dasher: I need a hammer. A letter opener. Anything. This is put together like a safe.

Earl: (*Enters and rushes to Meyer*) My God, Mr. Meyer, what happened to you? My God.

Sitter: He wants you.

Dasher: (*desperately pulling box apart*) He was mad, Earl. He was going to kill us.

Earl: (*listening to Meyer whisper*) What, Mr. Meyer? Yes, sir. I have the envelope. Yes, sir. He wants me to open this.

Dasher: What envelope? Give it to me. Give it to me. (Opens and reads) I Malcolm Meyer being of sound mind. You know that's not right.

Sitter: Give it to me, Dasher! Give it to me! (*Pushes Dasher against box and takes the letter*) Earl, he leaves you his seat on the exchange.

Dasher: You are now a rich son of a bitch, Earl.

Earl: I don't want no money, Mr. Meyer. Mr. Meyer? He is dead!

Sitter : My God!

Dasher: (*Finally opens box. It is empty*) I got it open!

Schlong: (*Reads ticker tape*) Assorted Technologies just lost its government contract. Call everyone before it's too late.

Dasher: (*Runs to his phone*) If it's not one thing it's another. Hello, Oscar. This is Dasher. Sell Assorted Technologies. I don't care what it looks like on paper. I know, I know what your report says. No, I'm not some sort of peace freak. Just sell it. Just do as I say. I'll talk to you later. (*Hangs up the phone as everyone stands frozen over the body of Meyer. Picks up phone again, calls*) I have to hand it to Meyer, he could really tell a loser when he saw one. (*back to phone*) Hey, Bunkie, you have Assorted Technologies, American Nuclear, Poomingdale's? No,not Bloomingdale's. I would really lighten up on all of it if I were you. Hey, sell the shit out of all of it....

(*Blackout*)

THE HISTORY OF DENTISTRY: PART 4

(THE ROOT CAUSE)

By Art Mayers, 2007

The original play debuted as "Open Wide" in 1986 and toured in Whitefield and Bath. It has suffered several rewrites to evolve to its present form. The initial inspiration came from a newspaper article about an Austrian dentist who practiced ventriloquism on his patients.

Cast of Characters   (original 1986 cast)

Klaus Dooblesprachen…. Middle aged Austrian dentist, David Benford

Kvetch Dooblesparchen… his wife, Tootie Van Reenan

Inge……………………..their daughter, Trish Johanson

Frau Washenrinse………the patient,   Jean Percy

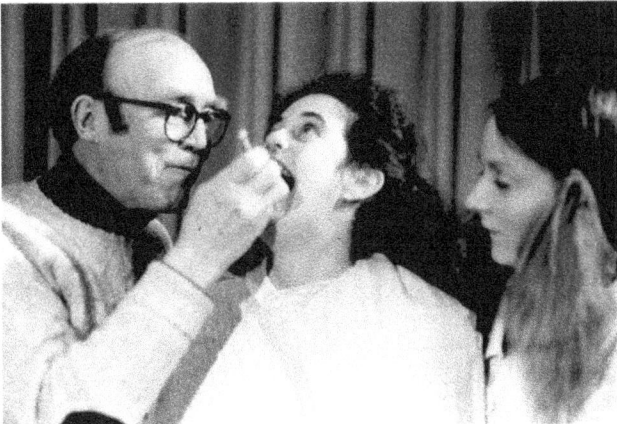

David Benford, Jean Percy and Trish Johanson, *Open Wide,* 1986

SCENE 1

(*We hear the sounds of bird calls, at first quiet, then building to a cacophony merging with the sounds of a cuckoo clock. Lights come up revealing Herr Dr. Klaus Dooblespracken doing warm-ups by the window. They are jerky but also gain in energy until he finally stops and stares into space. Kvetch, his wife, enters and begins to prepare breakfast.*)

Klaus: Come, Kvetch! Come and look at the sunrise. Come look at the greens as they change to blue as they change to yellow and red.

Kvetch: (*Long pause.*) Cereal or eggs?

Klaus: Did you hear what I said? (*Pause then staring again.*) It is a sparrow. (*pause*) No, no, no. (*Runs and gets bird book and binoculars.*) No, no, no. (*Looks at book then through the glasses a the number of times.*) No, it's a ruby-throated nuthatch.

Kvetch: There are Cheerios or cornflakes.

Klaus: (*excited*) I said it is a ruby-throated nuthatch.

Kvetch: We don't have nuthatches. The Cheerios are fresher than the cornflakes. The cornflakes are soggy.

Klaus: I know a nuthatch when I see one. Come look for yourself.

Kvetch: There is no such thing as a ruby-throated nuthatch. Close the window. You already have a cold.

Klaus: (*closes the window.*) Now, look.

Kvetch: Very well. (*She looks out window and shrugs.*)

Klaus: There by the wall.

Kvetch: That is not a nuthatch.

Klaus: A sparrow?

Kvetch: It is a seagull. (*Returns to her work.*)

Klaus: (*irritated*) What's the difference? What's the difference anyway?

Kvetch: I wish you would not open the window like that. We are trying to conserve fuel. Things are not as cheap as they were.

Klaus: I need the fresh air.

Kvetch: The air is putrid.

Klaus: I need the exercise.

Kvetch: Beat your chest with the window closed. You are such a stereotype. (*Pause as Klaus looks out the window.*)

Klaus: There is a terrorist in the garden.

Kvetch: There are no more terrorists.

Klaus: Yes, over there by the wall. He has no legs but he is a terrorist all right. Propped up over by the birdbath.

Kvetch: I am pouring the milk.

Klaus: Kvetch, Come share this moment with me. The sunrise, the seagull, the terrorist propped up by the birdbath.

Kvetch: I don't have the time. And neither do you, Klaus. Herr Schmidt is due any moment. We are totally unprepared for another difficult day, and you are not helping one bit. Besides, there are no more terrorists.

Klaus: There are terrorists everywhere.

Kvetch: Come and eat your breakfast.

Klaus: Eggs.

Kvetch: What?

Klaus: (*loudly*) I want eggs.

Kvetch:You don't have to scream.

Klaus: I am not screaming.

Kvetch: Your Cheerios are on the table.

(Enter Inge dressed in ballet tights.)

Inge: Guten tag, Papa. Guten tag, Mama.

Klaus: Will you stop that German gibberish? You'd would think we lived in Germany, for God's sake.

Inge: *(coming down stage and beginning ballet warm-ups, to audience)* This is Austria, time, the present. German is still our national language.

Klaus: Don't you think I know that?

Inge: Then I should speak German, Papa.

Klaus: Speak American like I do.

Inge: Yes, Papa.

Klaus: I try to provide for you with the work of my hands. I do the best I can. This is not a nice world we live in. The least I can expect is that I can pass on my values to my children.

Inge: *(continuing exercises)* Your values are wrong, Papa.

Klaus: What should that matter? Kvetch, back me up for God's sake.

Kvetch: Cheerios or cornflakes, Inge?

Klaus: Christ's sake.

Inge: Cheerios, Mama.

Kvetch: Take your father's before they get soggy.

Inge: Danke, Papa.

Klaus: Christ's sake.

Kvetch: Your father needs extra support today.

Inge: Poor Papa.

Klaus: Yes, poor Papa.

Inge: I love you, Papa.

Klaus: I'll take cornflakes.

Kvetch: Anything you say, dear.

(*The doorbell rings. The cuckoo clock goes off and everyone is thrown into a panic.*)

Klaus: How is it so late?

Kvetch: Herr Schmidt is here.

Klaus: I never take patients before nine.

Inge: It is 9:30, Papa.

Klaus: Where is my whistle?

Kvetch: Eat your cornflakes, dear.

Klaus: My whistle!

Inge: Here you are, Papa. (*She hands him the whistle. He blows it. They began to transform the room into a dentist's office complete with chair, instruments, laughing gas etc. They change clothes into whites, while at top speed.*)

Klaus: (*blows whistle*) Checklist, Inge.

Inge: (*gets checklist*) Checklist, Papa.

Klaus: Chair?

Inge: Chair, Papa.

Klaus: Instruments?

Inge: Instruments, Papa.

Klaus: Drill bits?

Inge: Drill bits, Papa.

Klaus: Spare drill bits?

Inge:(*to audience)* Later I would see this as an attempt to control Mother and me through excessive regimentation.

Klaus: Spare drill bits!

Inge: Spare drill bits, Papa.

Klaus: X-rays, Kvetch?

Kvetch: The film has been polluted.

Klaus: X-rays, Kvetch!

Kvetch: It has been exposed to light.

Klaus: I ask for x-rays and what do I get? You think I should hire a dental assistant with some sort of fancy degree so she can prance about with the lead blouse and keep proper inventories? I should hire some trained person off the street, that's what you think? You think I am some sort of idiot who has no family to exploit? Do you? Admit it. You want us to starve to death for a few lousy x-rays, don't you, Kvetch? Well, you are dead wrong. Who's the first patient?

Inge: Frau Washenrinse, Papa.

Klaus: Frau Washenrinse? That old rag. Pass. Who's the first patient?

Inge: Herr Schmidt is first.

Klaus: Then send in Herr Schmidt.

Kvetch: Frau Washenrinse called me, directly. She is in terrible pain. Her root canal is leaking.

Klaus: Send in Herr Schmidt.

Inge: But, Papa!

Klaus: Are you the receptionist? I asked your mother.

Inge: Mother is right.

Klaus: I am not interested in right and wrong. I am a dentist. I am here to survive. You are here to survive with me. I went to the university for seven long years to get my practice. I am not throwing in the towel now. Send in Herr Schmidt.

Kvetch: Herr Schmidt has not yet arrived.

Klaus: Then send in whoever has arrived. I am losing income every moment we chitchat.

Kvetch: Whatever you say, Klaus.

Klaus: Your mother and I sometimes don't see eye to eye. (*Calms himself as he prepares the tools.*) Who is she sending me?

Inge: I suppose whoever is in the office.

Klaus: You are a good girl, Inge.

Inge: You are killing her, bit by bit. You know that.

Klaus: Whom am I killing? What?

Inge: You are killing your good and faithful wife.

Klaus: Kvetch? She can take care of herself. I'm the one who is the victim around here.

Inge: You hurt her. Every day you take a little more of her flesh.

Klaus: I have enough problems keeping bread on the table.

Inge: She hates you.

Klaus: I will not have you talk of your mother in this way. Kvetch hasn't a hateful bone in her body.

Inge: She can't stand to look at your face.

Klaus: Inge, I will not have you speaking of your mother behind her back. Your mother is the salt of the earth. She is not a sniveling teenage nun.

Inge: (*crying*) Oh, Papa. You are the cruelest person on earth.

Klaus: Come on, Inge, cut it out. Don't be a baby. Dental assistants don't cry.

Inge: Papa, you are such a hateful beast.

Klaus: I know, I know, but can't you save it for later. Herr Schmidt will be here any minute.

Kvetch: (*enters*) Frau Washenrinse to see you, Doctor.

Klaus: (*whisper*) What did I say?

Kvetch: (*whispers back*) She is in terrible pain. She will pay through the nose.

Frau Washenrinse: (*enters holding mouth*) Guten tag, Herr Doctor.

Klaus: (*politely*) Good morning, Frau Washenrinse. Would you have a seat? You did see the sign on the waiting room door?

FW: Nein, Herr Doctor.

Klaus: For your information we speak English in this office.

FW: Das is sehr schern, Doctor.

Klaus: (*taking bib, swirling over her head, and tying it extra tight*) We insist upon it!

FW: Very well, Doctor. My English is rather rusty.

Klaus: Then work on it. What seems to be the problem, Madam?

FW: Pain. Terrible pain.(*putting finger in her mouth*) right here!

Klaus: Where?

FW: Right here !!

Klaus: But, Madam, I fixed that tooth. Last week I believe.

FW: Sie sind a blunder maken.

Klaus: I said no German...

FW: That was not German.

Klaus: Then what may I ask what are you speaking? I worked on that tooth last week.You spent a fortune here last week.

FW: Und die andern…

Klaus: Madam, I must insist. Who can understand such gibberish?

FW: The week before that. I have come to you every week with such pain. It is always the same. You give me the gas. You make me laugh. You put your hand in mine mouth. I am feeling better. I am happy all the week. Then on Monday, again...

Klaus: What?

FW: The pain. The terrible unbearable pain!

Klaus: I must say your English is improving, isn't it, Inge?

Inge: Your English is much better, Madam.

FW: Doctor, please tell me! Why have I no relief from the pain?

Klaus: You have heard of a temporary filling?

FW: Ohhh! It is the pain again.

Klaus: Well, there is such a thing as a temporary root canal.

FW: Oh! The pain is too much. Please, Doctor, take the pain away from me. I beg of you.

Klaus: Inge, the gas.

Inge: Yes, Papa.

FW: Thank you, mein Doctor. (*Klaus slips the mask over her face. She begins to giggle.*) Haa. Haa. I feel like a leaf. Ha. Ha. I feel like a daisy. Ha. Ha. I am a little squirrel. Ha. Ha. A baby girl in the daisies. I am young. Ha. Ha. Hopscotch. Hopscotch. Soda, mit rye. Ha. Danke, guten danke, Doctor, you are such a good doctor.

Klaus: The needle please Inge. (*injects FW with huge needle*) Does that hurt?

FW: Nein, Herr Doctor. It is feeling good. Ha, Ha.

Klaus: (*sitting down and picking up a magazine, reading*) The radio please, Inge.

Inge: Yes, Papa. (turns on radio, pre-recorded message)

(*The following material all happens somewhat at one time.*)

Radio: this is Radio Free Europe coming to you with the news of the world, brought to you in special English. And now the news. Prime Minister Klimt of West Germany today welcomed the neutron bomb to Berlin. Groundbreaking for the new totally automated missile system was made today. Special champagne flown in from New York State was provided as thousands of onlookers cheered the American Secretary of State who declared today to be Neutron-Free Tuesday...

FW: Such a silly boy you are...Ha...Ha ...my frock falls in the mud..ha.ha.. so young and so pretty. Pity. Ha. Ditty, kitty, kitty me. Pity me. Why so young? Why the flowers? Why the daisies?

Inge: (*aside to audience*) Later he would claim that his methods were medically sound. That Frau Washenrinse had no clinical complaint. That she would return if in fact she were completely toothless. I cannot say. I was a simple child. He appears so patient. So resigned. Is it I who makes him into a beast? Boorish. Cruel. Is Mother the victim or the protagonist? I hate him, the swine. Why does he raise his voice to us? Make us feel like animals? What must he think to be such a man?

Klaus: Inge. (*Motions that she should change the station. Viennese waltzes come on. Inge dances to the music. Klaus exits.*)

FW: Ah, music. I hear sweet music. The music of love. Da,da,dee,da. (continues to hum.)

Kvetch: (*enters carrying suitcases*) Inge, I am leaving.

FW: (*still trance-like*) Oh, don't leave me. Not now. I have just tasted life. We hardly know each other. We are still in love. We must learn to trust each other, fully hold each other's trust.

Kvetch: I packed my bags.

FW: Those are not your bags. Those bags are full of nectar. My sweet juice from which you shall make sweet, sweet honey.

Inge: (*to Kvetch*) What will papa do?

Kvetch: Who cares about him?

FW: Oh, my darling, I care. My love is not a passing thing. I shall only love once in this life. One cannot run out on the love of a lifetime.

Inge: Besides, Mama, those are not your bags.

Kvetch: Who cares. He owes me something. He owes me for this life of poverty. This life of misery. This life without end...

FW: Amen.

Klaus: (*re-entering*) Inge, where is your mother going?

Inge: Leaving you, Papa.

Klaus: Kvetch, please prepare Frau's bill. You cannot leave without money.You will need bus fare.

FW: I should not leave you for all the money in the world.

Klaus: Leave after lunch, Kvetch. Where is lunch anyway?

Kvetch: (*her resolve having waned, picks up bags and exits to waiting room.*) Sheis.

Klaus: (*calling after her*) Besides, Kvetch, those are my bags. Inge. (*Motions to her to change stations*)

Radio: Today, the last steel girders that support the Eiffel Tower were removed by workmen wearing rustproof suits.

FW: Voices. I hear voices. Voices in the night.

Klaus: Inge. (*Indicating a change, returns to music*)

FW: Music, such sweet music.Da, da, dee, da. (*etc.*)

Klaus: Inge. (*She shuts off radio*)

FW: (*coming out of it*) The music?

Klaus: The orchestra has gone home, Madam.

FW: The voices. Where are the voices?

Klaus: The musicians have gone to bed.

FW: Where am I?

Klaus (*to Inge*) Get the bill. (*Inge exits*) You are with me to Frau Washenrinse. You are with Dr. Dooblesprachen.

FW: Where is my pretty dress? What are you doing?

Klaus: We are preparing your bill, Madam. How is your pain?

FW: (*feeling her face*) I have no pain. I have no pain. Danke. Herr Doctor. Danke.

(*Kvetch enters followed by Inge*)

FW: (*to Kvetch*) Your husband is such a good doctor. H e with me miracles work. Was wunderbar fabriken das Gott Maken ist.

Klaus: Please, Madam you are slipping. The English. Remember the English. Please pay on the way out.

FW: (*exiting*) You must promise me, Doctor. I shall have no pain. I cannot stand the pain.

Klaus: As far as I'm concerned you are cured.

FW: Thank you, Doctor. Thank you. (*exits Kvetch follows her out.*)

Inge: Papa, you are a beast.

(*Blackout.*)

SCENE 2

(*The same scene as in the first case. Inge enters in pajamas, pours a glass of orange juice, walks downstage, addresses the audience*)

Inge: We skip ahead several years. Our family emigrates from Austria two steps ahead of the secret police, CIA, FBI, and Frau Washenrinse. Unfortunately, two steps were not enough for the Frau who follows us to the New World. Father has not changed his ways although retirement has given him a new perspective, however skewed, of the world. Mother has still not found the will or wherewithal to leave him. And Frau Washenrinse, the same. Yet here he comes, the master. (*She exits.*)

(*Enter Klaus who goes by the window and begins exercises. Enter Kvetch who goes about preparing breakfast as in first scene.*)

Klaus: Ah, the morning here. So fresh. The brilliant light of a new day in the New World. Come share with me, Kvetch. (*pause*) The colors. The reds, the blues, the New World greens. (*pause*) Kvetch? (*Long pause*) I hear birds in the garden.

Kvetch: Close the window, you will catch a cold.

Klaus: I thought we had resolved this. You are to drop what you're doing, which is drudgery at best, and respond to my enthusiastic call for you to come and see it, whatever it is. Well…

Kvetch: I thought you outgrew that. Haven't we put something behind us?

Klaus: We are talking more. We are expressing our feelings.

Kvetch: You are as needy as you ever were. "Come see the terrorists, come see the nuthatches, come see the dawning of a new day." There were never any nuthatches. They were always seagulls.

Klaus: There is terror in the world.

Kvetch: You just want me to give in. I don't have the time.

Klaus: Not even for old time's sake? There is plenty to see. There is light, colors. There is fresh air. Yesterday, there was a dead seagull, all wet, its feathers matted together. I didn't tell you. I didn't call you to look.

Kvetch: Good.

Klaus: You see how considerate I am.

Kvetch: You've always been considerate. Just needy, that's all.

Klaus: A good bargain, all in all.

Kvetch: How much do I gain from such consideration?

Klaus: Depends on how you look at it.

Kvetch: And how much do I lose from the neediness?

Klaus: You shall see, Kvetch. I am a changed man. People are tired of the absurd. They want some new heroes. I plan to be the prototype of the new hero.

Kvetch: Cereal or eggs?

Klaus: The heroic. We are all waiting for some great heroic gesture.

Kvetch: Well?

Klaus: We are still waiting.

Inge: (*enters*) Frau Washenrinse is in the waiting room.

Klaus: That old bag.

Kvetch: The new heroic is it?

Klaus: Don't look at me like that, Kvetch. Your mother has no faith in me, Inge. All right, send her in.

Inge: What of the chair? The instruments?

Klaus: We are in America. Things are less formal here.

Inge: As you say, Papa.

FW: (*enter FW, looks for chair, Klaus indicates chair. She sits*)

Klaus: What seems to be the matter, Frau?

FW: My cleaning.

Klaus: Speak up, Madam, I am not an ear doctor.

FW: You forgot my cleaning.

Klaus: Inge, the chart please. Hmmm. It says here you had a cleaning yesterday.

FW: I have sensitive gums.

Klaus: Have you ever heard of the toothbrush?

FW: I am filthy rich.

Klaus: (*becoming irritated*) That's not all you are.

Inge: Papa, remember, the heroic.

Klaus: Thank you, Inge. Open wide, Madam (*Begins to pick at teeth while humming*) Hmmm. Hmmm.

FW: (*garbled*) An animal is always an animal.

Klaus: What it was that, Madam? (*removes hand*)

FW: An animal is always an animal.

Klaus: Whatever you say, Madam.(*lurches*)

FW: Ohhhhh.

Klaus: What is it, madam?

FW: You hit a nerve, you beast.

Klaus: It is only tartar, Madam.

FW: Tartar, my ass. I know a nerve when you hit one. You are a Hun and a disgrace to your profession. (*Klaus starts to lose it.*)

Inge: Papa, don't.

Klaus: (*going behind her, trying to hold his temper*) May I tighten your bib, madam? (*making motions like strangling*)

FW: The pain. Give me that gas. I beg of you.

Klaus: Anything you say, Madam. (*grabbing the mask*).

Inge: (*aside*) Patience is a difficult virtue. The more it is practiced, the greater the potential for its loss.

Klaus: There you go, Madam.

FW: (*She begins to tremble, then with a muffled laugh she tries to say something.*)

Klaus: Yes, Madam?

FW: Ha, ha, ha. My shot, ha, ha, my shot, Doctor.

Klaus: Anything you say Madam. Inge, Madam's shot.

FW: Shall I hear the voices? The music?

Klaus: Of course, Madam, the voices. (*Inge hands him the needle.*) Thank you, Inge. (*jabs her*) The radio please, Inge.

FW: I shall hear that sexy voice, won't I, Doctor?

Klaus: Of course, Madam, only the very best. (*to Inge*) I am doing great, right, Inge?

Inge: So far so good. (*Turns on radio.*)

Radio: This is the voice called Radio Free Europe broadcasting in special English. And now the news. Terrorists have again struck a major oil depot in the South of Clanesistant, More than 70 people are feared dead. Latest reports. (*Static: Klaus bangs radio*) Latest reports.(*Static, bangs again while FW continues to giggle.*) Latest reports (*Bangs and then throws off table.*)

FW: The voices. Where are the voices?

Klaus: (*imitating the radio*) This is Radio Free Europe broadcasting in special English. Today we shall have a frank discussion on the meaning of freedom.

FW: I hear the voices. So rich. So slow. So sexy. (*Klaus begins monologue in the middle of her speech*) I see the daisies. White, the petals are white. The center is our sole yellow. The blue. My frock is so white and blue. There is some red. Where is the red? The red blood. My red blood. He talks so slowly. The grass is so green. It is cool. The air is warm. I should not worry, he says. The blood always comes the first time. The daisies. I should not let the blood touch the daisies. Not the first time. Mother should not see the blood on the frock. I hear his voice. I should not worry. I love you he says. I will always love you. I believed him. The first time should not be the last time. Not the last time. Never again. My poor frock. My poor bloody frock.

Klaus: What is freedom? We asked our leaders. The NATO bloc of countries, emblematic of the cause of freedom. But we asked ourselves, what is it to be free? After all, who does not make demands on our freedom? Is there not always some country that insists on being given gas, being put in a stupor. (*Begins to use ventriloquism to have voice come from speakers*)

Inge: Papa, please do not do this!

Klaus: What do we do when one country visits another country every day of its life and demands illicit drugs? What if that country is ugly and fat and wears outlandish hats and has bad breath?

Inge: Mother, please come quickly.

Klaus: What if she sits in a chair like an over-stuffed whale and insists on reliving her gross ugly fantasies?

FW: My music, where is my music?

Klaus: Inge, do something. (*Inge begins to hum a waltz and dance to it*)

FW: Yes, das is gut.

Klaus: What if that old country won't shut her filthy mouth and insists on hearing Viennese waltzes for her wrinkled perverted ears? Who is then free? (*Moves to tighten her bib*)

Inge: Mother! Mother! Mother!

Klaus: Who can be free in such a world? When did it all go wrong? When did rituals replace purpose? When did chatter fill in for conversation? When was love replaced by anger and resentment? I once thought I could find people's souls by looking in their mouths. I found only plaque. People are fortresses and there is nothing behind the walls. Our shells becomes thicker every day. Our true feelings never reach the surface and if they find a hole, a tiny crack, they come out bent like a pretzel. Frau Washenrinse, you are the same as I am, you old perverted dishrag. You and your voices. I am only the vehicle that carries you to your dreams. All right, give us back our feelings, whoever you are. This is Radio Free Europe broadcasting to the world in special English. This is to announce we have lost our insides. Let us feel our anger. Let us feel our love again. We won't put up with this any longer. Make us free! Free! Free! (*choking FW*)

Kvetch: (*enters*) STOP! (*Klaus stops in mid-motion.*)

FW: What is happening? The pain. I feel no pain. Doctor, what have you done?

Kvetch: I must excuse my husband. He doesn't know what he is doing.

FW: He doesn't know what he is doing? Your husband is a genius. I am cured. I am so grateful. Please, how much is my bill? I have not felt better in my life.You have my blessing, Herr Doctor, Frau Dooblesprachen. (*exits*)

Inge: (*runs to Klaus and hugs him*) Papa, Papa, Papa.

(*Blackout*)

SCENE 3

Klaus: *(Same thing as before, except kitchen is a total mess. Klaus again by the window)*Ah, the morning air. Come and look at the sunrise, Kvetch.

Kvetch: Cereal or eggs?

Inge: *(aside)* As you can see our situation has deteriorated. Many things have changed but just as many have stayed the same. Klaus has given up ventriloquism, although his speech about freedom, I believe was his finest hour. The voices coming from everywhere, " All right give us back our feeling, whoever you are. This is the voice of America broadcasting to the world in special English. This is to announce, we have lost our insides. Give us back our feelings. Whoever you are. Let us feel our anger.Let us feel our love." Great stuff if you ask me. All right, the ventriloquism was just so-so, but…

Klaus: Inge!

Inge: Frankly, I would rather relive the past than just talk about it all the time.

Kvetch: Frau Washenrinse called.

Klaus: What does she want?

Kvetch: She said she had an appointment.

Klaus: An appointment? Didn't you tell her I'm retired? I am no longer practicing dentistry on any level, at any time, to any one.

Kvetch: She considers herself an exception.

Klaus: I have sold my chair. I've given up my tools. I no longer speak with an accent.

Kvetch: She doesn't care. She trusts no one but you.

Klaus: Call her up and tell her I no longer have a license to administer scheduled drugs.

Kvetch: You have a closet full.

Klaus: I beg of you. Tell her the laughing gas is stale. That I no longer have sodium pentothal. That I'm under investigation. That I am a quack, a proven incompetent.

Kvetch: She knows all that.

Klaus: Tell her that I practice the most brazen form of cruel and abusive charlatanism.

Kvetch: She knows.

Klaus: Tell her that I refuse to perform in any way. That I won't listen to her perverted stories of her ill-spent youth. That I'm not in the mood for her cries of anguish and despair. That I shall not sit by and have her pay through the nose for services unrendered and mis-performed. That I won't be her patsy, her buffoon, her lackey, her slave, no matter what promises of fortune she lays at my feet.

Kvetch: Her appointment is at nine.

Klaus: It is already 9:30.

Inge:(*Enters*) Frau Washenrinse is in the waiting room, Papa.

Kvetch: Your father claims he has retired. He has given up gimmicks and gadgetry.

Klaus: I simply refuse to work for a laugh.

Kvetch: Or money, but not matter. (*Enter FW*)

FW: Ohhh.The pain. The terrible, unbearable pain.

Kvetch: Your father believes in a Spartan existence. No frills, no extras.

Klaus: I rely on character.

Kvetch: Which he lacks.

Klaus: And circumstance.

Kvetch: Which he avoids.

Klaus: And timing.

Kvetch: Of which he has no sense.

FW: Ohhh. My chair. Where's my chair?

Klaus: You see, Inge, how the Frau's English has improved.

FW: Where is my chair?

Klaus: Inge, find Madam a chair.(*She does, FW sits.*)

FW: Thank you, Inge. As least someone here cares for those in pain.

Klaus: I was just telling Inge how we no longer cater to Frau's every whim. How we have managed to extort enormous sums from you without resorting to special effects, comic pratfalls, expensive drugs, audiovisual flimflam, or overlapping segments of dialogue. I have explained our discovery that people require no further narcotic than the one with which they enter so that we serve merely to supply focus to their already bourgeois, decadent pastimes. If they wished to be moved...

Kvetch: Emotionally moved...

Klaus: Emotionally moved, they will find any excuse, so why beat our brains out.

FW: Please, Doctor. The pain. Can you do nothing for the pain?

Klaus: I have heard all this before. Kvetch, get my instruments. Not the whole bag. Just the bare essentials, if you will.

Kvetch: Yes, your Majesty.

Klaus: And hold all other patients.

Kvetch: In one hand, your Majesty. (*Exits*)

Inge: Well?

Klaus: Get Frau ready, Inge. We have also given up unnecessary dentistrial trappings. We have canceled subscriptions to all the fancy, la-de-da magazines that are out of date before they arrive, while maintaining back issues when the covers have not been torn or abused. The New Yorker is timeless if you only read the cartoons. Just the bare essentials. Travel light. Avoid entangling alliances. Always collect past-due bills.

FW: The pain, Doctor. The terrible, unbearable pain.

Klaus: (*Taps his feet waiting for Kvetch, long pause*) Yes, we have made life simple. (*Kvetch returns with bag, hands it to Klaus, who goes to the tools rejecting certain ones*) No. .. No... No..

FW: May I see?

Klaus: No need, Madam. Don't worry that we will use older damaged instruments. What you don't see won't hurt you. My hands are too shaky to use any picks or probes. (*Removes an enormous hypodermic needle*) Now, Madam, just relax.

Inge: Papa, Papa, not the needle.

Klaus: Don't bother me now, Inge. (*Jabs FW in arm*) There, okay, okay. Now just wait a moment. Things will be better now. You will feel pain but you will no longer care. Your pain will become your pleasure, your pleasure your only pain.

FW: Pain is pleasure.

Klaus: We have been through this before, Madam?

FW: Yesterday.

Klaus: So recently?

Inge: (*pleading*) Papa!

Klaus: What is it? Can't you see Frau is in a state of becoming?

Inge: But the needle? Papa!

FW: The flowers. Oh, the pretty flowers. Girls dancing for their joy.

Klaus: You see, Inge, there is nothing to be concerned about. Dance for Madam.

Kvetch: Your father no longer supplies the music. Frau dances to her own tune.

Klaus: I merely supply the text. Inge, dance for old time's sake. (*Phone rings.*)

Kvetch: (*answers phone*) Oh, my, Central America calling. It's for me.

Inge: (*dances while humming a Viennese waltz. Continues throughout the simulspeak*) Da, da, de,da....(*etc.*)

(*note: the following is simulspeak, i.e., each actor speaks his part at the same time as the others are speaking, going slowly and leaving pauses to let the other speeches bleed through-- the idea is to have fun with a mixture of the sounds and meanings without being totally cacophonic.*)

FW: The daisies, the beautiful daisies… flowers in profusion. So young, so very young, and yet so beautifully innocent. Strikingly innocent. And the handsome beaus. Always suiting where they may and June. I was their blossom, their tender bloom, to be sullied as they wont. But they won't if they don't dress in violet petals. As we pedaled here and there. The obscene bicycle rides not far from the suburbs near the power lines, electrical arteries pumping blood, my blood on my beautiful white things. Mother, why have you allowed me to make my own mistakes? You should have stopped their heat from entering me. A girl to be sotten by those young sots not yet drunken of life. Help me. Don't trust the thrusts, not so deep a peep into my private world, never to see a marriage bouquet, at 17, 16, 15, bang. I am banged up and no mother to wash away the blood, my first blood, my last blood from that damned spot. Out.

Klaus: Simplification. The gradual letting go of the needs. If there are no needs there can be no emotion. Bad emotions move to anger, to be displaced, misplaced without understanding. Anger, surging without control. The media was a mistake. Voice of America, outwardly calm, controlled, a peaceful world; inwardly striving, secretive, aggressive. The Voice of America was a mistake. I am willing to give up the past. That is growth through simplification. Why pursue negative energy? Nobody wants it. People won't tolerate it. Especially if they pay good money. To be abused, manhandled. Life is no musical comedy. Controlled development, a dash of sentiment, no forced denouement, stay away from the cute, the expected, television, the past, add a touch of the bizarre, the deformed, no freak shows mind you, this isn't a circus. Inge, Inge, Inge!

Kvetch: (*on the phone*) Oh, my, not the state department? Nicaragua. El Salvador. Guatemala. A Central America travel advisory. Cloudy with a chance of occasional shrapnel. Light bombing over the central and northern highlands. Cool in the mountains with partly mined infrastructure in the early morning giving away to mild strafing by the mid-afternoon. A mild terror front moving in from the south in the late afternoon east of Lake Managua. A boating advisory with interdiction of arms after sunset. The evening should be tepid in eastern sections with napalm bursts in the lower foothills. Intermittent shelling in all but downtown capital area for Tuesday. Of course. Thank you very much.

No, I didn't know this was free. A courtesy of the CIA. Emergency standby in the event of all-out covert war. But thank you all the same. Klaus, Klaus, Klaus! It was Nicaragua calling.

(*End of simulspeak*)

Inge: Papa, Papa, Papa!

FW: Where is my music?

Klaus: (*ready to explode*) Where ever is your music, Madam? The music stops at some time. We have no control over melody, harmony, rhythmicity. We have forsaken the electronic way. We are in a period of musical austerity. Haven't you noticed? All around you, Madam. Have you no ears? For better or for worse, we have cut the umbilical cord with the popular musical idiom. That goes for major and minor chords. You better have a song in your heart Frau because you won't hear it here. Do you understand, Madam. Not from me, not from the V Voice of America, and not from my family either.

Inge: Papa, Papa, please.

FW: I understand, you beast.

Klaus: The pain, Madam. You have forgotten. I have relieved your pain.

FW: The pain is gone.

Klaus: No more pain. Where is my thanks?

FW: Of course. You are thanked. If you would give me half a chance.

Klaus: Never mind. Just pay and leave. I am in no mood for plaudits. Just go.

FW: (*rising*) I am so thankful to you, Doctor, Fraulein, Frau Doublesprachen.

Kvetch: Dooblesprocket. We had it Americanized.

Klaus: Go ! Go! Just go.

FW: (*exiting, to Inge*) Emigration has done your father wonders.

Inge: I know. (*FW exits*)

Kvetch: If you think I am fixing your lunch after such a display…(*puts on a straw hat*). The days when I would happily whip up a little snack of sausage and buns are gone. Or a plate full of yesterday's noodles for a noontime gnosh. Forget it. The midday sliver of liver pate with a slice of half sour pickles and a side order of sour cream. You must be kidding. You can cut your own mustard, honey.

Inge: You equate mother's acquiescence to your every whim, often on the most trivial, minor issues such as lunch, as respect for you.

Klaus: That is all under control now.

Kvetch: Nothing has changed. (*Picking up her bags*) except that I no longer make your lunch.

Klaus: Where are you going?

Kvetch: Nicaragua.

Klaus: Why would you want to go a disease-ridden, Marxist, war-stricken, tropical sewer of a country like that?

Kvetch: For a breath of fresh air. For a change. I am sick of the fat cats.

Klaus: Fat cats? See any fat cats around here? You think Frau Washenrinse has made us fat cats? Besides, Kvetch, those are my bags.

Kvetch: Sheis. (*Exits. Klaus goes to window*)

Klaus: Inge, come here. (*Gazing out the window*)

Inge: What is it, Papa?

Klaus: The sky. It is so spectacular.

Inge: Not now, Papa.

Klaus: The clouds. They change so peacefully. Change can be peaceful. Reassuring. You are missing something beautiful. Inge, come here and watch.

Inge: No, Papa.

Klaus: Today, we have taken a step forward.

Inge: Speak for yourself, Papa.

Klaus: I have found peace in the center of the storm. I have found a still rock in the middle of a landslide. Quiet changes have come to pass.

Inge: You say that every day, Papa. Nothing ever changes.

Klaus: The clouds. The camels are now flying geese. Watch with me, Inge.

Inge: No, Papa, please don't, Papa.

Klaus: Look at the jet trail. Cutting down into the yellows and gold..

Inge: I want my own life. Let me go, Papa.

Klaus: It is dimming now. You have missed this moment. It was so beautiful.

Inge: Please, Papa, please don't do this to me.

Klaus: This is the moment! Can't you see? This is the moment of inner fulfillment and peace!

Inge: Oh, God! (*Covering her face and crying*) Oh, God!

Klaus: It is all gone now. (*Turning from the window*).

Inge: I will go away to college, Papa. I will go away for good. I shall get a Masters, a Ph.D. if you ever put me through this again.

Klaus Sharing can be beautiful.

Inge: Not your way. Not your way, Papa. (*Kvetch enters and runs to her.*) Oh, Mama. He is still a brute.

Kvetch: You shouldn't do that Klaus. It's all right to do your sunsets to me, but Inge.

Klaus: Inge can take care of herself.

Kvetch: I am hard ened to your ways, but Inge is still a child. Inge, please leave the room. I have something to say to your father, alone. (*Inge exits. Long pause*) Frau Washenrinse is coming back tonight, Klaus. I know what you are going to say, "I won't see her, what other dentist sees patients at night?" I know I have told you this before, but Klaus, you are not like other dentists. Now Klaus, I'm not going to tell you what to do. Neither am I going to make idle threats. I'm not going to remind you that we are here in America, clinging to work visas by the thinnest strand of red tape. I'm not going to tell you the consequences of blowing it with the IRS, the FBI, and the Secret Service. We are that close to getting walking papers from the entire Western Hemisphere.

Klaus: Surely, you exaggerate.

Kvetch: That close. I assure you. I'm not merely talking about being disbarred, defrocked, dismembered, drummed out of the corps. I am not threatening long term sentences in federal penal institutions, passing dark listless hours in a narrow cell on the bottom bunk, under a snoring moron who talks television with his one channel, child molesting mind. I am not going to bring up knocks on the door at all hours, subpoenas, interrogations, extraditions, renditions, deportations to unknown countries ruled by ministers of health and finance who don't know a WaterPik, from a temporary filling. I'm not going to dredge up the memories of packing, wrapping, and crating our remaining belongings. Or of waiting for moving men to put another dent in the medicine chest, another scratch on the lowboy sideboard. I won't mention the lost telephone deposits, damaged security checks, the unwanted parting gifts from neighbors who never dreamed of talking to us until they saw the gas disconnect on our underpaid service lines . I will not insist that you see Frau this evening.

Klaus: What other dentist sees patients at night?

Kvetch: You are not like other dentists.

Klaus: So you remind me.

Kvetch: On the other hand, I shall not offer you any inducements, prizes or favors. I am beyond that. I am not that desperate that I should flirt and make lewd suggestions to bring you around. I find no real need to throw my body at you, since you no longer crave or respect my seldom offered and ill-received concessions to your steadily waning appetites. I am no longer your sex kitten. Why should I? Nicaragua. In Nicaragua we might renew ourselves. Our sweating bodies might find their way to gather in something resembling passion under the palms, in air-conditioned hotel rooms after rationed showers. I would give it a chance. But you refuse. You would rather be forced onto the sidewalk than take the high road. You talk of the heroic. There is nothing heroic about conviction, excommunication, deportation. When will you ever take our moves into your own hands? Nicaragua might be our last chance. Klaus! Please I beg of you. We don't have many continents left.

Klaus: Let me think about it.

Kvetch: Oh, Klaus.(*Throws her arms around him*) Nicaragua. And Frau?

Klaus: Send the old bag in here.

Kvetch: Oh, Klaus, Klaus, Klaus. There is hope.

Klaus: I said I would think about it.

Kvetch: *(exiting blowing him a kiss.)* Nicaragua.

(Klaus stands by the mirror taking on various poses, George Washington, Napoleon, Patton. FW enters, moves down stage to audience.)

FW: He doesn't have the slightest idea. There you go. Assume a stance, a posture, a pose. Spit on the street. You can't make a hero out of a deadbeat. You have to earn your strut. What a clown! You have to change your character before you can change the world. Get off the tit, you middle-aged cabbage. A Brussels sprout, boiled and fleshy, ready to fall apart with the push of a fork. Some hero! A hero needs something, a cause perhaps. Something to rally the soft flesh around.

Kvetch: Nicaragua *(from offstage)*

FW: Nicaragua, perhaps, perhaps Nicaragua.

Kvetch: NIC-A-RA-GUA!

Klaus: (coming out of daze) Frau! What are you doing? Talking out there. Poignant asides. Have you no shame?

FW: You were posing.

Klaus: That is a lie. What kind of a peeping patient are you?

FW: Heroes are not cut from such logs. Always the cute, the rhetorical, always straining for a laugh, a twist, a nuance without substance, something from your bag of clever wordplays. Where is the heart here? Hero, my ass.

Kvetch: (*peeping in*) Nicaragua!

Klaus: Sit down, Madame. I said sit down.(*FW sits*) Now what seems to be the matter?

Frau: The pain, the terrible, unbearable pain.

Klaus: That was this morning.

Frau: My cleaning, you forgot my cleaning.

Klaus: That was after lunch. It is now 10 o'clock in the night.

FW: You chipped my tooth, you brute!

Klaus: We have been through this today. Don't you patients have any integrity?

FW You have no other patients. You and your family are totally dependent on me for your survival. Without me you would have no professional credibility. You would be all alone in a world without support from a legitimate way to maintain your household. Without me you would be a vagabond, a tramp, a dentist without a cause. I am the only one who keeps you from the great void beyond. I alone maintain your foothold on respectability. I am your lousy meal ticket, BOZO!

Klaus: Kvetch, Kvetch, come in here! Quickly!

Kvetch: (*with a rose in her mouth*) Nicaragua?

Klaus: Kvetch. Don't ask questions. Get me my tools. Get in here. I'm going to do something that I should have done years ago.

Kvetch: Nicaragua?

Klaus: I am actually going to fix Madam's teeth.

FW: No! (*Tries to rise, Klaus restrains her*)

Klaus: Sit down, you old bag. Go Kvetch, quickly. Before I change my mind.

FW: You won't get away with this.

Klaus: Don't be so sure.

FW: A coward is a coward for life.

Klaus: A man can change himself.

FW: A Brussels sprout is a thing forever.

Klaus: I can see the sky now.

FW: Another act, another charade. You could never fix my teeth. Not so that they would stay fixed. There would be a mistake. It might take an hour, overnight perhaps, but there would be a flaw in your work.

Klaus: White clouds and a clear blue sky.

FW: A leaky root canal.

Klaus: Guitars playing softly. Sweat running off my back.

FW: Plaque jammed under a molar gum.

Klaus: Coffee drying under the hot, tropical sun.

FW: A spot of chipped enamel on the flank of an incisor.

Inge: (*enters*) Nicaragua, Papa?

Klaus: Nicaragua.

Inge: Not another one of your tricks? Nicaragua?

Klaus: Nicaragua. Now get me the laughing gas.

Inge: Yes, Papa.

Klaus: No, on second thought, I want Madame to see a real dentist at work.

FW: My gas.

Klaus: No gas, Inge.

FW: My needle, my sodium pentothal.

Klaus: No Inge. No needle. This one is cold turkey.

Inge: Cold turkey, Papa. Oh, Papa, Papa, Papa. (*hugging him*) You have broken the cycle. Cut the cord. I am so happy for you. I love you.(*Exits in a hurry.*)

Klaus: (*turning back to FW*) Now, Madam, what seems to be the problem? There, I see something.(*Jamming his hand into Frau's mouth*) a logjam of spiritual turpitude.(*mimes an extraction*).

FW: Oh! My music. Where is my music?

Klaus: Nicaragua.(*Jams his hand back in her mouth*)

Kvetch: (*Entering with her bags*) What, Klaus?

Klaus: (*pulling hand out again*) Warehouse of human insolvency. Nicaragua!

Kvetch: Nicaragua, Klaus?

Klaus: Nicaragua!

FW: my music! Where is my dance? (*Gasps as Klaus re-enters her mouth.*)Agh!!

Inge: (*enters*) Nicaragua, Mama?

Kvetch: Nicaragua, Inge! (Inge starts to dance wildly across the stage)

Klaus: (*as if pulling out her entire mouth*) Sanctuary of pitiable petulance! Nicaragua!

Kvetch: Nicaragua!

Inge: Nicaragua!

FW: Agh!   Arrg!

Klaus: What is it, Madam?

FW: AGGHHHHHH! NICARAGUA!!!!

(*Blackout*)

SCENE 4

(*Klaus sitting head-on chest in wheelchair*)

Klaus:(*mumbling*) Nicaragua. Nic...a..ra..gua.. Ahhhh.

Kvetch: (*enters and goes to kitchen*) Cereal or egg?

Klaus: Nica.. goddam.. poopala.

Kvetch: Come on, Klaus. You know what the doctor said. You have to keep up your strength. Work on your fiber. Carbohydrate loading. Bed rest, lots of it, and a proper diet. No sugar, milk fats, nuts or citrus fruits. No red meat or shellfish. Some thin fish when not oily. No mackerel or tuna fish. Klaus? (*Walks over and feels his pulse*) Klaus, you scare me sometimes. Inge!! (*Klaus jumps, startled*) Where is that girl? It's time for your vital signs. Inge? Klaus, if you would only listen to reason. Dr. Reason. Your condition is debilitating yes, post-Central America Shock Syndrome. Seeing the world as it really is. You have a right to feel as you do. But there is also something in your system. An amoeba, a parasite, a pinworm wheeling about but we all had that. We all retched our guts out. but, Klaus you didn't come out of it. You didn't overcome. Two weeks in Paradise and you came home a vegetable.

Klaus: :Nic..a.. rot...you.. are.

Kvetch: At first you were so alive. How romantic it was. The palms, the sun, the beaches. Coral atolls swept by the trade winds. And how you rose to the occasion. You were a real husband, a real father to Inge. You and your $12 camera shooting everything in a bikini, and some without. You went so wild. Bare breasts and Marxism. How you loved the contrasts.

Klaus: Nica... titidom.

Kvetch: Where did it all go wrong, Klaus? I was just beginning to feel something for you, Klaus. Don't think I didn't, just because I would turn to the wall when you came on to me, doesn't mean that I didn't feel the profound change in you,

Klaus: No nooky..a..ra..gua.

Kvetch: And then there was Ernesto. You were so jealous. Sweet little old Ernesto. Coming to the hotel, reading us poetry. The flowers were for you too, Klaus. Red roses are for men too. Ernesto was just there to welcome us, to make us feel at home in his country. And you insulted him. You said you have

110

no use for his Canto su Liberasion. The poem was not written for me. So what if he called me his North American kitten. He was only making a political point. That is no reason for insulting his Canto su Liberasion. It took him six years to write his Canto su Liberasion. Long before Inge and I set foot on his sweet mother soil. So you're jealous of me and Ernesto? So what? That is no reason to be jealous of Inge and Ernesto. Ernesto is 65 years old. A well preserved 65, I admit. And how old is Inge? Eighteen years old. Inge is a mere eighteen years old.

Klaus: Son of a bitch.. agua.

Kvetch: And what is your response, when threatened by a Latin half your size and 10 years your senior? So what if he is a General with a police force the size of a small army at his beck and call? He would never use force to get my love, or get Inge's love for that matter. What do you do? Old horny on the first day Klaus Dooblesprocket, North American, ex-dentist on the eve of a new life in a tropical paradise? You get sick. You become moribund and catatonic all in one giant gesture of sexual insecurity. What if you did vomit every forty minutes for six days? That is no reason to insult an important General in a country that has enough problems. When will you ever learn not to over-react (*pause as she looks at his motionless body*) I love you, Klaus. Inge still loves you. And Frau...

Klaus: (*eyes open wide*) Wash..n...rinse.

Kvetch: If you didn't want Frau to come with us you should have said something before she got on the plane. Sometimes, Klaus, you're not clear in stating your feelings. If you didn't want Frau to share our hotel room you should have been more open with her. Frau is human. She is not the kind of person to be totally closed to discussion or plain talk. Sometimes I wonder about you, Klaus. On the one hand you maintain a level of professional proficiency. You can still hold the WaterPik. At least you can hold your instruments. You have a degree, several degrees, and yet when it comes to interpersonal... (*enter Inge*) Good morning. Inge, could you take your father's vital signs?

Inge: Mail call, Papa. Mail call, Mama. (*Holding out a packet of letters*)

Kvetch: Cereal or eggs, Inge. (*Spooning Klaus cereal that he doesn't take*)

Inge: Looks like more letters of sympathy from around the world. I never knew Papa was so well, well, well...

Kvetch: Respected?

Inge: Yes, Mama.

Kvetch: Could you check your father's temp?

Inge: (*opening letter*) $1000 from the Unified Peoples Fund.

Kvetch: He seems awfully cold this morning.

Inge: Here's $500 from the Serbo Croatian Dental Disability Fund.

Kvetch: He is so very sweaty about the temples.

Inge: $500 from Save the Hopeless. Poor Papa, more honored in sickness than in health (*putting letters down*) Nothing from Ernesto, Mama.

Kvetch: Please check your father's vital signs.

Inge: Not today, Mama. (*going to the sideboard and taking Klaus's cereal*)

Kvetch: Just because you were transformed in Paradise doesn't mean you can't pull your weight with the family. I speak for your father when I say that none of our opinions have changed just because you're engaged to a foreign dignitary.

Inge: The Cheerios are soggy.

Kvetch: Just because you are a queen in the socialist bloc doesn't mean you can't do a few capitalistic tricks here on the home front. And don't think your Marxist credentials are going to get your room back. If Ernesto wants to stay the night, it's the Holiday Inn.

Inge: All right, Mother (*she goes and gets the thermometer blood pressure gauge.*) That reminds me, Dr. Reason called to say he couldn't make it. He is sending a paramedic.

Kvetch: What would a paramedic know about post-Central America Shock Syndrome. (*She walks to kitchen area.*)

Inge: I don't feel the pulse. Poor Papa is dead. I'm sorry I let you down, Papa. I know you wanted me to be a ballerina. I know you wanted me to have a degree in biochemistry. I know you wanted me to be at your side handing you the water spritzer and dispensing injections of fraudulent narcotics to unwitting patients. You wanted me to be your little kitten not a sex idol for the Latin socialist bloc. I failed you, Papa.

Klaus: Nargg. (*Changes the position of her hand on his wrist*)

Inge: Not dead, Mama. Pulse normal, Mama. Temps normal, Mama. Mama, why did he give up his career? Why did he stop being a dentist?

Kvetch: (*washing dishes*) You remember. You were here. It was his decision to fix Frau Washenrinse's teeth once and for all. "Log jam of spiritual turpitude, warehouse of human insolvency, sanctuary of pitiable petulance." His finest hour if you ask me.

Inge: No, he gave up long before that. Long before our flight from Austria, long before the ventriloquism.

Kvetch: Ah, the ventriloquism. A brilliant idea. If only Klaus had practiced more. Taken lessons somewhere. Gotten certification.

Inge: Don't you see? The ventriloquism was an act of desperation. He was already drowning.

Kvetch: Your father never fell from greatness .It was a steady decline, a slide. You have to realize that your father was nothing before we met. Just another pimply-faced dental student. He knew nothing of women.

Inge: And everything changed after he met you?

Kvetch: You have to realize you can't make a silk purse out of a sow's ear. Not overnight, anyway.

Inge: And you made him into a real man?

Kvetch: Your father was a late bloomer. I came along in the bud stage...

Inge:... and sort of clipped.

Kvetch: Your father was never much of a ladies' man. He tried to please too much. He tried to meet my every need. Women don't like that. Every other need is good enough. Anything more gets oppressive. He was just lucky I was there to unfold the petals. Without me who knows what would have happened?

Inge: A virgin, Papa was your virgin?

Kvetch: Someday you'll understand.

Inge: And you, Mama?

Kvetch: Let me put it this way. I had known all I wanted to know long before I met your father.

Inge: But what of his career? What of Papa's career?

Kvetch: There is more to life, Inge, than one man's hopes and dreams.

Inge: Where did it go wrong? Where did it all go wrong?

Kvetch: You will have to ask your father about that.

Inge: But father is a vegetable, Mama.

Kvetch: Don't talk that way, Inge. I wouldn't count your father out yet. I have known him too long for that.

Inge: But look at him, just look at him.

Kvetch: Times have been tough before. I guess I'm an optimist by nature.(*Doorbell rings*) Oh, my, who could that be? Ernesto. Ernesto has come in his Russian jet. My goodness, just look at me. Such a mess! This will never do.

Inge: First of all, Mother, it is I who am engaged to Ernesto.

Kvetch: Where's my Guatemalan dress? I'd better brush up on my Spanish (*bell rings*) oh! Ernesto! I am coming. (*Exits*)

Inge: In the second place...(*goes to replace thermometer, FW enters in paramedic uniform, Inge returns to talking to Klaus who sees FW and becomes agitated.*) Papa, you shouldn't be so critical of Mother. After all, a vacation is meant for change. We wouldn't have gone to a country in revolution if we did not want some change in our lives. Remember, you were the one looking for a heroic gesture.

Klaus: (*seeing FW goes rigid in chair*) Ancient-agua!!

Inge: Ernesto may be a little wizened but his heart is young. He may be more Mother's age, and I can see why an older man might be threat to you...

Klaus: (begins to move chair in small circles) Nica...loonie.

Inge: Ernesto may be a little offbeat, the fatigues, the beret, but he is fighting for the poor. That may seem strange to our middle-class ears, but his revolution is for the masses...

Klaus: Nica...Augehen!

Inge: Papa, you are slipping into German.

Klaus: Nica... IAufgenoutamysightbittefrauhava cuckoogenhenauf. (*goes into complete panic.*)

Inge: Frau, it's you.

FW: Your poor father. When I heard, I rushed right over. He seems quite agitated. Don't worry, Inge. I am trained. I took a crash course at the University. It was a breeze, though I did crush three dummies practicing CPR.

Klaus: Nica... (more German gibberish.)

FW: Your father starts all of his sentences with Nica. That is strange.

Inge: Is that bad?

FW: Everything is bad. Paramedics never get a call unless things are bad. We only take cases that real doctors wish to avoid. Emergencies and that sort of thing.

Inge: Most times he is almost comatose. I haven't seen him so agitated.

FW: I can fix that. (*Goes into bag and brings a can of laughing gas*)

Inge: Frau. My God, are you licensed?

FW: I am a paramedic. This part comes to me naturally. It is only a harmless laughing gas. (*She jams on the brakes of the chair which stops Klaus dead in his tracks and then slaps the mask on his face*) There you go, Bozo, a little of your own medicine. Now for the sodium...(*pulls out hypodermic needle*)

Kvetch: (*Enters in peasant dress*) Oh, Ernesto you have come for... Frau Washenrinse!

Inge: She is certified, Mama.

FW: There you are, my dear. (*jabbing him with the needle*)

Klaus: There you are, my dear. So sweet in your little dress. Your knee is like a little sweet potato. So we sit by the shores. The sandy shores with your heels making angels in the sand, my hands working upwards under your embroidered violets, touching down, fluffy stuff, hairy where your underwear should be. Too much for my young gun, glands and pump, pump, hot into my shorts, all the hot juice on the sticky sand. And to hold onto what I got, hot, shot, looking into the sun gliding over Mount Blankenschwartz.

Kvetch: Mount Blankenswartz? You never took me to Blankenschwartz. I was never at Blankenchwartz with you.

Klaus: Blankenschwartz and spent, on my shorts, eyes sharing, hearts feeling, together, never, never, again.

Kvetch: You took some Fräulein, some little sweet thing to Mount Blankenschwartz before my time and had some soul meeting. Some sunset heartsmertzing before I got the hook in...

FW: I told you he was a beast.

Kvetch: And every time you drag me out to see one of your lousy sunsets to recall one of your pre-pubic sluts.

Klaus: Greta.

Kvetch: Greta. She even has a name, Greta.

Klaus: Greta...agua. Great, Greta. Nica.. great, Greta, sweet stuff agua.

FW: He's coming out of it.

Kvetch: It's about time, the beast.

Inge: You're a beast, Papa (*doorbell rings*)

Inge and Kvetch: Ernesto!

Kvetch: Well go answer it.

Inge: Me?

Kvetch: He's your fiancé.

Inge: But you found him. It is to you that he has dedicated his Canto su

116

Liberasion. It is you he calls his little piña colada.

Kvetch: Can't you see I still have business here?

Inge: With Papa?

Kvetch: No woman would ever leave the man who still has the slightest memory of another woman. The slate has not been erased. If there is still the slightest glimmer of something sweet in that catatonic consciousness, until that is gone, until there is nothing but me paralyzing the soul of this vegetable, Ernesto will have to wait.

Inge: (doorbell) Ernesto is waiting, Mama.

Kvetch: The point is, Inge, picking apart a man is a long and backbreaking job, and I'm not sure I want to start again given my age and Ernesto's age and the fact that Ernesto may not be around long enough to finish the job. No, with all his faults Klaus is my baby. I have my vegetable. I might as well keep him on my platter. Ernesto was just a little parsley on the side. You go.

Inge: I can't, Mama. I only wanted him because you wanted him. What would I do with an old romantic socialist poet here in the, in the, in the ...

FW: Suburbs?

Inge: Thank you, Frau. And Ernesto wouldn't be happy here without volcanoes and counter-revolutionaries. Nobody knows how to hate the rich here in the, in the, in the place where we live.

Kvetch: (doorbell) Go, Inge, go. (Inge exits)

Klaus: Kvetch, Kvetch.

Kvetch: I am here, my love.

Klaus: I see them. Come here, my dear.

Kvetch: What is it?

Klaus: I see them so clearly.

Kvetch: What my dear?

Klaus: The terrorists.

Inge: (*rushes in crying*) He is gone. Ernesto is gone.(*Telephone rings.*)

Kvetch: I'll get that.

(*Simulspeak*)

Klaus: Come, Kvetch, come see the terrorists. So much more efficient than those silly nuthatches. So much cleaner, marching two by two, four by four into the setting sun. Come look at the colors, how beautiful, the yellows changing to orange, to blue, to green. Come Kvetch, share one moment, that is neither you or me. Outside ourselves, without needs, without demands, without our own privately colored picture. A world outside ourselves joined in ourselves with our eyes. Listen to the clump, clump, of those terrorist shoes. In the garden, the sound of the last nuthatch before its flight south. The touch off our hands held together, fingertip to fingertip. Two souls facing outward into the world shared. That is all I ask. That is all I dream for.

Inge: Oh, Mama, Mama. He has left us. Our poet has gone. We have sent him away from the sub… sub.. suburbs. Back to his socialist junta, beneath the volcano. I have been passed over again, Mama. I have not been taken, not been loved. Even the old men reject me, Mother. I never became a dancer. Poets can respect a dancer but not a girl who couldn't make it through one semester at a junior college. Mother what shall I do? I have no future here in the sub…sub.. suburbs. What can I do? Sell real estate? Work at the Dairy Bright? My life is over, Mother. My Marxist dream has passed me by. I am one lost chick.

Kvetch: China calling. China on the line. Yes, yes… What did you say? A capitalist revolution! Chickens going to market! Small business entrepreneurs! Zero population growth. A number 18 on every menu. Well, it sounds just marvelous. And you want people with technical know-how? Poultry engineers. Family planners. Disenfranchised yuppies. My, that is a breath of fresh air. And medical persons. Dentists, dental assistants, dental records specialists. So tooth decay is on the rise. I know, you have Coke now. Medics, paramedics, all combinations of medics… Well, let me ask… China on the line, dear. (All faces are turned to the east.) What shall I tell them? Klaus… Klaus Klaus! China on the line.

FW: (*entrance to imaginary boy*) Oh, silly boy, why I would you want someone like me? I am three times your age. It's the uniform. It's just a standard issue, paramedic white. You are after my drugs? I know you boys. You don't want a woman for love. All you are after is to get high and pass out in some lady's arms. They warned me about your type in paramedic school. Your popping veins, your dilated pupils. 911 freaks. That's what they call your type. You've been downing all day and want to come up, so you expect some one like me to come in, needle in hand, looking for romance and shoot you up any old way you want. You think paramedics are all alike. That's where you are mistaken. Just because we are all white and badges doesn't mean we don't want sex like everybody else. We are not drug machines you know.

Klaus: Fake! I am a fake! (*Ventriloquism begins. Voices from place speakers*)

FW: I told you this was good stuff.

Klaus: I am a liar, a fake, and a fraud.

FW: How sweet the sound.

Klaus: Send back the money. Return all the checks.

Inge: Mama, Papa is throwing his voice.

Klaus: I cannot accept the life savings of all those well-intentioned persons.

Kvetch: What is he saying?

FW: He is making a clean breast of it.

Inge: The sounds are coming from everywhere.

Klaus: I was never sick. I was always pretending. Listening for your pity, and then when the money started...

FW: We have you, you scoundrel.

Kvetch: What is he saying?

Inge: It's the ventriloquism. The ventriloquism is back, Mama.

Klaus: I couldn't resist the attention. The vital sign taking.. The spoon feedings. You hung on my every word. Then I stopped talking. That brought me more power. More control.

FW: I should call the police. Mail fraud is a serious crime.

Kvetch: Is it your father talking, Inge? What is he saying?

Inge: He's so much better at it this time. The sounds are coming from everywhere.

Klaus: I learned how to slow my heartbeat. Raise my body heat. Withhold my pulse. I lived on your fear. I thrived on your concern.

Kvetch: What is he saying, Frau?

FW: (*on telephone*) He's spilling the beans. He's making a clean breast of it. Hello, police.

Inge: Oh, Papa, Papa. What a talent! You are so good. You can make the walls talk.

Klaus: Kvetch, I'm so sorry for deceiving you. The Nica...Nica... stuff was pure invention. It's me in here, just little old Klaus Dooblesprocket, your childhood sweetheart.

Kvetch: Sweetheart? Who said sweetheart?

Inge: The china closet, Mama.

FW: It was that beast you call a vegetable. Hello, Sergeant...

Klaus: Come, kiss me, Kvetch.

Kvetch: (*suddenly catching on*) You! You are throwing your voice!

Inge: Isn't it great, Mama?

FW: The beast is at it again.

Klaus: I am a liar, a fraud, a charlatan. Kiss me, Kvetch.

Kvetch: You aren't dying?

Inge: Of course not, Mama, he is a genius.

Kvetch: Tell me the truth, Klaus.

Klaus: Kiss me, Kvetch.

Kvetch: Stop the ventriloquism. Talk to me you.... You... you...

FW: Beast!

Kvetch: Thank you, Frau.

Klaus: I am healthy. I'll send back all the money. All I want is for you to forgive and forget.

Kvetch: Why you are talking out of the gas range, Klaus? Talk to me out of your own mouth.

Klaus (*talking out of his mouth*) I am a fraud. I am a healthy, middle age, retired dentist, and I love you, Kvetch.

Kvetch: And Greta?

Klaus: Greta was just a thought of the moment. Kiss me, Kvetch!

Kvetch: Ernesto! Where are my bags? Ernesto! Where is he, Inge?

Inge: (*shocked*) Mama?

Kvetch: Ernesto! Wait for me. It's your capitalist sex kitten. Wait for me. (*Exits*)

FW: (*on phone*) Yes, Sergeant, he has confessed, to mail fraud, yes...

Inge: Papa, you were wonderful. Your ventriloquism was first rate. (*Hugs him*)

Klaus: (*getting out of chair*) Where is Kvetch?

Inge: She is going to Ernesto, Papa. It's just you and me now, Papa.

Klaus: You can't have your room back, Inge. Where is Kvetch?

Inge: Gone with Ernesto, Papa. Teach me, Papa. Show me how you do it.

Klaus: You should be in college, Inge. Learning how to find a man.

Inge: I want to learn everything you know, Papa. I want you to be my university.

Klaus: Find Kvetch for me, Inge find her. I need her, now (*roughly*) go, go find her.

Inge: Papa, you are a beast! (*Exits on the run*)

Klaus: (*slumps into chair*) What have I done? They are all gone. I am lost. Who shall take care of me now? Who shall love me now?

FW: Address? 271 West... Just a minute, Sergeant. I'll call you back in a minute. (*Hangs up the phone. Goes over and picks up the gas tank*) Klaus, oh, Klaus Dooblesprochet...

Klaus: (*looking up despondently with a touch of fear*) What is it, Frau?

FW: The gas is fresh... Sweetheart.

(*Blackout*)

Mildred's Chorus

About "Mildred's Chorus"

Mildred is a fighter. Having lost her husband, Jimmy, some twenty years earlier, she struggles on to keep her love of the "old" music alive, in spite of almost total rural isolation. She imagines that the children, who used to come and perform, still come and practice after school for the annual Christmas show for the parents. For her, Jimmy, her valued "light man", is still in the back room waiting to assist her. One remaining neighbor still calls to check up on her to make sure she doesn't slip totally into her imaginary world.

One day David comes to sell Mildred a magazine subscription and finding out that she has a piano suggests that his group called "Garbage Boats" needs a place to practice. Mildred, thinking that she has tapped a new pool of young talent, opens her doors to the punk movement, assuming that she will be able to "direct" again. Not only is she assaulted by a new wave of musical values she is robbed by the group tough, Tommy. When she discovers the discrepancy and threatens to expose them she is bound, gagged and held hostage. We expect the worst for Mildred and she probably would have lost the contest and her life if she had tried to escape. But Mildred fights with the love for her musical values and in the end, she is triumphant.

For the play I draw upon my own childhood contact with Mildred and Jimmy and my ambivalence towards those Christmas shows. I add to that my own frustrating experience with a local Maine homegrown teenage rock group and finally a news item about an elderly woman held hostage for several weeks who, when released, had no regrets, and "Mildred's Chorus" is born.

Cast of Characters (Waldo Theater 2008)

Mildred...... a woman in her seventies , Ellie Busby Hinds

David......a teenage boy, a drummer , Hugh Valiatis

Bruce …David's brother, leader of the group, Cole Christine

Tommy ……the tough guy, band member, Dennis Boyd

Tammy ….Tommy's girlfriend, Lily Christine

Cole and Lily Christine as Bruce and and Tammy, 2008

SCENE 1

(The set may vary, represents a rural New England parlor as it might have been furnished m the fifties and allowed to deteriorate to the present. Exits to interior and exterior, the main feature being an upright piano and bench. Enter Mildred. She is m her seventies, white-haired, plainly dressed. She is carrying four mugs of cocoa on a tray which she places on a coffee table. She counts the cups to be sure of the number.)

Mildred: *(calling back towards the interior)* Jimmy? Do you want cocoa? *(long pause, no answer)* I didn't think you would … that leaves four … just the right number. Arthur, Mary, Susan, and Billy …children like cocoa … when they get home from school. … maybe a little extra sugar. *(starts back towards interior, stops)* No, their mothers would not approve , would not approve … sugar is bad for children … but, oh, how they love it … maybe just a little. *(exits, returns with a sugar cup, adds a little to each one, then a heapmg teaspoon)* Oh, what the heck … there you go, my little geniuses. *(stirs each one carefully)* There … there … there … there. What does a mother know? As long as it's hot. *(puts spoon down and begins to rummage in the piano bench)* Jimmy? Where is my music? Jimmy, do you hear me? *(closes the bench and goes to interior exit)* Jimmy … I said … did you hear me? Jimmy?! *(returning to the piano)* Deaf as a post . inner resources … inner resources ..I must muster my inner resources. *(rustling papers on top, of the piano)* You might as well be dead, all the help you are … at show time you'll be here … running the lights, serving cookies to the parents … at show t:ime you'll be here … you better be. *(gives up search on piano top)* Jimmy, you are one heck of a disappointment to me … hiding things. The desk. *(goes to desk and resumes the search)* Jimmy … JIMMY, WHERE HAVE YOU PUT MY MUSIC? You'll have the neighbors popping by. Busybodies … a woman can't scream at her husband without a neighbor thinking the worst. *(finds a manila folder)* What about this? *(removes sheet music)* There we are … there we are … "Old Man River" , "Tea. for Two"…"Bicycle Built for Two" … an easy one for Billy … no flats or sharps for my little Billy boy ••• "Somewere Over the Rainbow" , "Someone to Watch Over me" All here. What did I tell you, Jimmy? Manila folder … Organization. One needs organization, especially in show business. *(begins to sing)* "There is someone I am longing to see, I hope that" he … she." (*begins to address imaginary Arthur, standing to her side*) You should say she." You are not longing to see a he, are you, Arthur, my boy? … change it. (*takes a pencil and makes change*) "There is someone I am long1ng to see, I hope that she turns out to be … someone to watch over me." Jimmy! My fingers are cold. (*rubbing hands*) Will you do something, for once? Sorry, Arthur. (*resumes with piano*) "I'm a little lad, who's lost in the wood, I know I could, always be good, to the one who'll watch over me". (*clears throat*) Grrhmmmmmmm My voice is going. (*goes to cocoa and takes sip, then to imaginary Susan*) I'm taking a sip, Susan. I hope you don't mind. You won't mind. (*Returns to the piano*) where were we?... Okay... "I know you may not be the man some..." That's wrong. This song is wrong for you, Arthur... I told you that... You're going to have to change the you to I .. (*Changes with pencil*) "I know I may not be that man some, girls think of, as handsome, but to my heart you carry "... Shoot. (*Mark music again*) "I know I may not be the and some, girls think of, as handsome, but to your heart out carry the key." Pretty conceited little fellow you are, Arthur my lad. (*puts head and hands*) Old Man River... You'll sing Old Man River. Let your sister sing Gershwin. (*Writes note*) Mary to sing," someone to watch over me"... there. (*Telephone rings*) Jimmy?... will you answer that?... (*rings again*) not in the middle of a rehearsal. drat. (*Goes to the phone*) yes... yes, Betty, I am fine... no, not so much pain... and Bert?... no, no one likes intensive care... (*impatiently*) yes, Florida would do him a world of good... it could kill them, the humidity is awful I hear,... I am fine... no, I have everything I need … the pain is quite bearable. Listen, Betty, I have some guests... no, young people... of course I know them, what do you think?... they are just children... I must be going, their cocoa is cooling rapidly. Goodbye... say hello to Bert.goodbye. (*Hangs up the phone*) Now, where were we? (*Takes up cocoa cup, feels outside, takes a sip*) sorry, Mary... it's cold. (*Exits, returns with sauce, begins to pour)* busybodies... what good are neighbors?... old, sick neighbors, dieing neighbors. Jimmy? The cocoa is getting too cold for my little stars... Jimmy?... must I do everything?... this cocoa needs heating. Now then, (*goes to music removes a sheet)* this is a big day for you, my little Arthur. "Old Man River"... this is your big chance for stardom. (*Sits at piano*) let's skip to..." you and me, we sweat and strain, bodies all aching and racked with pain, tote that barge"...this is the good part... "lift that bale, get a little drunk and you land in ja..el. " No, Arthur not jail it is ja..el. You go right down to j..el. Of course I known you know how to read... you are in the fifth grade, sixth, I'm sorry... but the way it goes is j..el. Why?... because it sounds right. Now try again to get a little drunk and you land in j..el." If you can't reach the note will change the key (*raises the key*) okay, "get a little drunk and you land in J..el." Now you're flat... of course you can sing in the key,... it's no different, just higher, and the sharps and flats are different. You sing along with me. "Get a little drunk and you land in j..el." Still flat... well, I'm sorry, we can't all be perfect all the time... you are flat so let's try again... I know you're tired... school must be exhausting, but our show is just a week away. Your father and your mother will be here. Susan and Billy's mother and father will be here too. God knows who else might come to hear us. You don't want to be an embarrassment. Let's just try it my way. Yet a little drunk... you have to start a little higher, we change the key. Well, you're not with the piano, what can I say... no, you can't sing just by yourself... it's called a cappella and it's for professionals. No, you can't quit... let's start over... no, you can't sing at low. I'm telling you Arthur, you can't quit now (not Condor). That would ruin the whole show. (Knocking) Jimmy, when you get the door? Jimmy... home my God, the cocoa. (Rushes to exit) Arthur I'll be right back.,For God's sake,Jimmy get the door! (*knocking. She returns carrying cocoa ,*) It's burnt.. You can't quit on me, Arthur. This is show business. (*knocking*) Jimmy! My hands are burning , (*knocking. She goes toward exterior exit*) For goodness sake, who is it? (*opens door still with pan in hand*) Who is it? (*opens door*) Art hur?

David: Hello.

Mildred: No, it's someone else. Ohhh, this cocoa is hot.

David: Hello.

Mildred: Hello, come in, not Arthur. (*rushes to put cocoa down*) Let me put this down.

(*Enter David, a rugged teenager, sixteen, carrying a briefcase*)

Mildred: You must excuse me. I'm trying to do a thousand things at once. You're not Arthur.

David: No, I'm not Arthur.

Mildred: I knew that. You didn't look like Arthur at all. Arthur is chubby. Besides: you're older than Arthur. Arthur is in grade school. A very temperamental boy. Do you sing?

David: No, mam

Mildred: Of course, you sing. Everybody sings. Music is part of our souls. Without music, there is no soul. Everyone is musical. It just doesn't always get to the surface. Sometimes it needs a little help.

David: I play the drums.

Mildred: There we are. What did I say? You are musical. What is your name?

David: David.

Mildred: And I bet you're not a quitter, are you David?

David: I am not a quitter, mam.

Mildred: Not like Arthur. It's just a lack of maturity, that's all. Talent isn't everything. It's stick-to-itiveness that counts. Do you want some cocoa, David?

David: No, mam.

Mildred: It's hot. It's even burnt a bit. Come on.

David: I'm going door to door. I'm selling .....

Mildred: That can wait till later. (*Getting cocoa and pouring a cup*) All children go door to door. It's a good way of meeting people. Rich people, poor people, old people. It's good for young people to see how other people live. (*handing him the cocoa*) There you go. Everything is show business, anyway. (*David sips*) Is it too hot?

David: No, mam.

Mildred: It's too sweet. I put in extra sugar.

David: It's not too sweet.

Mildred: It's burnt. I could tell by the smell. I was preoccupied with a sensitive performer. Arthur. You may know him.

David: No, mam.

Mildred: You can't be sensitive in show business. They'll chew you up. Everybody makes mistakes. Nobody is perfect. There is bound to be somebody telling you you're wrong. Even if you're right, you're going to be wrong to somebody. Isn't the right, David?

David: Right.

Mildred: And most times if it feels right, it is right. Unless it's the director that is telling you, you are wrong. Then you are wrong. It's burnt, isn't it?

David: Mam?

Mildred: The cocoa is burnt.

David: The cocoa is fine, mam.

Mildred: So what are we waiting for. (*Goes to music and thumbs through*) No…No…No Ah here we go, "Tea for Two".

David: Mam, are you interested in Grit. If, I should be moving on.

Mildred: Of course I am interested in grit. Persistence and grit. Have a seat. (*selects a sheet of music*) You know this one? You are young, probably not. We'll skip to the verse. "Picture you upon my knee, just tea for two and two for tea, just me for you and you for me alone…dear" There is a rest before "dear" It should be like a duet. You sing one line and I sing the next. What are you waiting for? You can't perform if you don't rehearse.

David: I have a lot more houses.

Mildred: Now you go, " Nobody near us to see us or hear us, no friends or relations on weekend vacations ... " Come on, you sit down here. I'll sing with you. (*He sits gingerly on piano bench*) "We won't have it known dear that we own a ...

David: "Telephone .. "

Mildred: ... dear." With the pause. That's the way, David. You have a fine voice. "Day will break and you'll awake and start to bake a sugar cake ... " Go ahead, your turn! Go ahead. Right there. Let me. "For me to take for all the boys to see." Now once again. "Day will break and you'll awake, and start to bake a sugar cake ... " Hit it!

David: "For you to take for all the boys to see ... "

Mildred: Now it changes. We will raise a family, a boy for you ... (*points to him*).

David: ... a girl for me."

Mildred: You've got it.

Together: " ... Can't you see how happy we will be."

Mildred: That was great. Just great. You're better than Arthur ever was. Arthur, Susan, Mary, and Billy put together. Jimmy! Come in here and listen to David. What's your last name?

David: Hutchins.

Mildred: David Hutchins. Jimmy? He's deaf as a post. Sometimes, I even forget he's there. Forget about Jimmy. Just one thing. Arthur never gets this right. I should change it for you right now. You see where it says, " for you to take for all the boys to see .. " We're talking about the cake that she makes for him, but the song isn't always sung my way so its says "you" instead of "me". You will want to change the "you" to "me" because you are taking the cake for the boys to see. It isn't logical that she is taking the cake for the boys to see. It wouldn't be much of a marriage if she takes the cake to other men. If you see, what I mean. Even though it says the men are just supposed to look at the cake, not eat it. It wouldn't make sense. It wouldn't be right, musically. That's just a fine point. Arthur never could remember to make the change. It was pencilled right on his score. So we'll just cross this out and put in "me" for you. Got it?

David: I should be going.

Mildred: Any questions.

David: Is this your piano?

Mildred: Of course, it's my piano.

David: My brother plays the piano.

Mildred: That's wonderful.

David: Except we dont have no piano. It's hard to practice without a piano. We have a group.

Mildred: How wonderful. What do you call your group?

David: Our new name is "Garbage Boats".

Mildred: How cute.

David: We used to call ourselves "We stink" But we couldn't get no gigs, so now we are 'Garbage Boats" There are four of us. My brother Bruce, his friend Tommy, and Tommy's girlfriend, Tammy.

Mildred: A quartet.

David: I don't sing. Only some harmony.

Mildred: You have an excellent voice.

David: We don't get to practice like we should.

Mildred: Where do you live?

David: On Hatch Hill.

Mildred: Come and practice here.

David: You mean it?

Mildred: Jimmy ,won't mind. I'll talk to him.

David: I got to set up my drums.

Mildred: Jimmy wouldn't hear a bomb if it went off beside him.

David: There are four of us.

Mildred: I like to direct four at a time. Four is a good number.

David: We don't need a director.

Mildred: Of course you do, everybody needs a director.

David: Tommy's not so easy some times.

Mildred: Just like Arthur. Come, let's practice one more time.

David: I have to go. Can we come tomorrow?

Mildred: After school?

David: We don't go to school no more.

Mildred: Then whenever.

David: Ten o'clock.

M~red: That would be fine.

David: Thank you, mam. (*exiting*) I forgot, do you want Grit? (*reaches for his paper bag*)

Mildred: (*closing the door behind him*) All the grit I can get. Remember, its" me" and not "you". (To herself) You do have a better voice than Arthur. And you don't have a temper. I can't stand oversensitive talent. It's so inconsistent. Brilliant one moment, dead the next. Give me a good dull-witted tenor and I can make him a star. (Sitting at the piano) I could make meatloaf into a star. It's all in practice, good direction, and getting the "you's" changed to "me's" (*playing*) "We will raise a family, a boy for you and a girl for me, can't you see how, happy we will be." Jimmy! Jimmy? What's wrong with you, Jimmy? We're directors again. I'm a director, again. (*Blackout*)

Ellie Busby Hinds as Mildred, 2008

SCENE 2

(*Same set as before. As the scene opens David, Bruce, Tommy, and Tammy are setting up their band equipment. They talk to each other, ignoring Mildred.*)

Mildred: (*enters with cocoa on tray*) Here we go! David, cocoa.

David: In a minute.

Mildred: Bruce?

Bruce: Mam?

Mildred: Cocoa?

Bruce: In a minute.

Mildred: Tommy?

Tommy: I'm busy.

Mildred: Tammy, it is Tammy?

Tammy: Yes, mam.

Mildred: Cocoa?

Tommy: Tammy!!

Tammy: Sorry, Mildred, I have to help.

Mildred: (*sitting at piano*) Just like children. Always busy. No time for good nutrition. I must apologize for Jimmy. He wanted to meet you all. He's not up for it just yet. He had a terrible night. He gets so excited ... New children. Not that he didn't like the old ones .. Arthur and the rest .... Whatever were their names? .. Susan ... Sisters and brothers ... Two families .. Neighbors ... We would have adopted them if necessary .,. We never did though ... It was never necessary. We had sheep, and

lambs and the lambs had lambs. We ate them . It never bothered me ...
You can't eat your own children ... You can't make a sweater or rug
from them either.

Bruce: (*Handling a heavy piece of equipment*) Watch out, David?
Don't bust up the furniture.

Mildred: (*playing a few notes, deeper in revery*) Chickens .. We had
chickens ... Arthur used to feed the chickens for us ... They would eat
the plums in the summer and the eggs were always sweeter for it. Billy
used to play down in the brook making little dams ... Fishing without a
hook ... He was fat in those days ... There weren't any fish, anyway.
Arthur would mow the lawn and I would make lemonade. Their parents
never missed them ... Never worried. I put extra sugar in the lemonade.
Arthur took care of all the animals after school. His mother bought the
eggs And I gave the money to Arthur. At Christmas time we would
have our shows. One day Arthur quit his job. He said his mother
wouldn't let him come. She said he was too old to take care of animals.
What is too old?

Tommy: Tammy, move your corner.

Mildred: Then Billy wouldn't come ... Susan and Mary only came at
Christmas, anyway ... Noone came. I had to cancel rehearsals. Arthur's
mother never said why. She could have called or told Susan's mother to
tell me. Did I say something? Did Jimmy do something wrong? Were
the eggs rotten? I had pride. lf she wouldn't say, I wasn't asking. Jimmy
and I worked. We had our own lives. We sold the sheep. There was
noone to help .. Jimmy got an electric lawnmower. He liked that ... lt
was too late for us, so Jimmy bought a lawnmower and we sold the
sheep. I should have sold the piano too. No more Christmas shows. No
Arthur to throw tantrums. They all quit. Just in one day .No one told us
why. lt would have killed Jimmy if he were a weaker man. We saw
them everyday, then nothing. They never gave a reason.

David: (*holding a power cord in front of her*) Twenty or thirty amps?

Mildred: What?

David: Do you have fuses or circuit breakers?

Mildred: Fuses, I think.

Bruce: We don't want to blow no fuses.

Mildred: Don't worry, Jimmy knows how to change fuses. (*taking out sheet music*) I picked out some nice songs: "Bicycle built for Two", "Clementine", "Tea for Two, A mixture of traditional and contemporary. I don't know what your folks like.

Tammy: They don't like music.

Tommy: We don't play for them.

Bruce: We are burning a CD.

David: People around here don't understand us.

Tommy: Dumb hicks!

Mildred: Music is a universal language. It's our souls making melody for our heart's rhythm. Together it expresses the harmony of living ..

Tommy: Tell that to my dad.

Mildred: We will. Of course, we will. Our concerts have always been well received. Jimmy on the lights. Me on the piano. The kids singing their little hearts out. I put the parents right there. You wouldn't think there would be enough room. We've never had to turn our audience away for lack of seats. Don't worry, you'll see.

Tommy: We don't play out.

Mildred: You've got no confidence. Show business is confidence. You need a good director. A good light person. Someone to pick your program. Here, Tommy, this looks like you. (*handing him sheet music*)
.

Tommy: (*pushes it back*)

David: We have our own music.

Tammy: It's mostly original.

Mildred: Wonderful. Less work for me. I'll work on interpretation.

Bruce: We do that.

Mildred: I can help arrange.

Tommy: Our songs are all arranged.

Mildred: I'll listen.

David: Can she listen?

Bruce: It don't make no difference to me. (*They take up their instruments. Tommy is lead guitar; Bruce on piano; David on drums; Tammy in front of the microphone for vocals.*)

Mildred: I'll be honest and tell you whether its good.

 Tammy: Why don't you just listen, mam?

Tommy: And don't say nothing.

Mildred: I'll shut my trap. (*buttons her lips*)

 Bruce: O. K. 1,2,3,4 .....

(*They play. The song may be chanted to a punk beat or some tune may be devised. The actor's should make an attempt to play the instruments but not well*)

"We stink! We're not talking bought body odor

We stink!

We don't smell, we're just plain bad

We stink!

Come down on your parents, come down on your folks. We're playing for bad times, we don't like sick jokes Come out of your closets with your sticks and your clubs. We'll beat on your carhood, we'll smash on your stubs

We stink!

We'll play on your windshield, we'll lay rubber for you. We'll stomp on your dashboard, we'll kill if you sue. We'll slash at your tires, we'll zippo your tank; We're not asking for much, just proof that we stank. We stink.

We'll sit on your vinyl, we'll pee in your ashtray. We puke on your panels, we'll get into your way. Don't try to run out, we'll melt down your keys; We're bad as we look, and not looking to please. We Stink!

We're not talking bout body odor

We Stink!

We don't smell, we're just plain bad,

      WE Stink, We stink, WE STINK! I!!!"   *(end song)*

Bruce: That's our title song.

Tommy: We usually throw a smoke bomb into the audience.

David: When we got an audience.

Tammy: Nobody comes no more.

David: Even our groupies have quit.

Mildred: You need a ballad.

138

Bruce: That was our ballad.

Mildred: I mean like" Summertime", or " Up a Lazy River", or "Bicycle Built for Two" (*telephone rings, she goes to answer*) or"Lady be Good" Hello, Betty.

Tommy: What does she know?

Mildred: How is Bert?.. Intensive care? .. Not again!... Hospitals will do it every time.

Tommy: Let's split.

Mildred: I'm fine... Just a couple of kids come over to play music ... Of course, I'm all right ...

David: I want to play, " Sucker's Walk".

Tammy: I don't know" Sucker's Walk".

(*Tommy is looking about the house, finds an envelop, opens it, takes out a wad of money*)

Mildred: I'm eating *fine. I've got plenty of eggs ...*

Tommy: (Whispering to Bruce) Hey, look .. (*Bruce comes over and examines the envelope. Tommy takes it back takes a number of bills and stuffs them in his pocket*).

Mildred: ... Just some kids. They have their own songs. No, I don't think it's Rock n' roll. (*turns as Tommy replaces the envelope. rolls her eyes to the group*) Yes, it is another generation. I have to get back to rehearsal. Say hello to Bert. Bye, Betty. (*hangs up then to the group*) They'll talk all day if you let them.

Tommy: We got to go.

Mildred: I want to hear more.

Tammy: You don't hate it?

Mildred: I wish to reserve judgment. More cocoa?

Tommy: We're going.

Mildred: Would you do me a favor? I can't get out. Could you pick up some things for me. You have a car.

Tommy: It's not running good.

David: Tommy! Sure. We can do it.

Mildred: Here's the list. Betty's husband is in the hospital. I don't want to bother her. It's just a few things. (*Gives list to David*) Let me give you some money. (*Goes to envelope, opens it, senses something is wrong but doesn't say anything*) There you go. Here's ten. Why don't you buy something for yourselves1 Some chips and soda. Come back and play something more. I want to hear your music.

Tommy: Come on, let's go.

David: What about the instruments?

Bruce: We can trust you, can't we, mam?

Mildred: Oh, you can trust me.

Tommy: I don't want no one playing my guitar.

Mildred: Don't you worry. Take five, as they say.

Bruce: O.K. Let's take five.

Tommy: Take ten.

David: Whatever you say, mam.

Tommy: Come on! (*they exit*)

Mildred: (*Looks in her envelope. Counts the money, once, twice*) Jimmy? (*Goes to her purse, looks inside without luck*) Jimmy! Will you come in here? Did you borrow any money? My social security. Did you take some of my paycheck? Did you take some grain money from me? No, you couldn't. You always pay by check. You keep such good records. The bedroom! (*exits to bedroom*) I told you to pay by check. (*returns*) I never misplace money. I never buy anything. I never go anywhere. (*goes to the drawer of desk, removes paper*) $175.60. It's always the same. (*counts money*) Eighty-five dollars and sixty cents. Ninety gone. I gave them ten. I gave them ten. (*puts money back on the table where it was. Stares at it, then becomes frightened*) Jimmy, oh Jimmy, Jimmy, Jimmy! Such nice children. They wouldn't. They couldn't. Not from the director. Not from their own director. Maybe, they want to fire me. They don't like the way I direct. No, no, show people are honest. I have hardly done anything yet. It's too early to be dissatisfied. They're just kids. Maybe they don't know about showpeople. Jimmy, for godsakes, come in here. I need you. (*she hears the car*) Back already? I'll ask them. I can't ask them. They did me a favor. I can't accuse them. They have my groceries. I need my groceries. They have my change. (*pause*) They didn't take it. They didn't take anything. I can't direct when I'm nervous. (*noise at door*) For godsakes, Jimmy, help me out! (*returns the envelope to its place*) Act, Mildred, you must act calmly. Act like you've never acted before.

Tammy: (*enters with grocery bag*) They didn't have no wheat crackers so we got saltines.

Mildred: (*seated at piano looking through sheet music trying to ignore her fears*) Saltines are fine, Tammy.

Tammy: (*exits to kitchen*) Where do you want the crackers?

Mildred: The counter is fine.

Tammy: The butter cost a lot so we only got one stick.

Mildred: Where are the boys?

Tammy: They're waiting in the car. They're drinking their ... soda. We bought corn chips. (*reenters*) Is that, O.K.?

Mildred: I want you to buy what you like.

Tammy: Bruce bought a beer. He's eighteen.

Mildred: I didn't know he was that old.

Tammy: Tommy's the youngest. He's sixteen. He's my boyfriend but. I am older than he is. Only six monthes. He drinks beer sometimes,too.

Mildred: So they're all in the car drinking beer?

Tammy: You're a hard too fool ain't you, mam?

Mildred: Call me Mildred.

Tammy: Mildred. There wasn't much change, with the deposit and all. (*takes some change and puts it on the desk*)

Mildred: Why don't the boys bring the beer in the house?

Tammy: They didn't think you would approve.

Mildred: I don't mind beer. I don't drink it, but I don't mind it.

Tammy: They're waiting for me.

Mildred: What about practice?

Tammy: They are kind of tired of practicing.

Mildred: They only sang one song.

Tammy: They're just sleepy.

Mildred: What about you? I have a great song for you here. "Over the Rainbow" from The Wizard of Oz.

Tammy: Oh, I don't sing solos.

Mildred: " .. Somewhere over the rainbow, blue birds fly. Birds fly over the rainbow, why, oh why, can't I?" It's in your range.

Tammy: Really, I couldn't.

Mildred: You even look the part.

Tammy: Really, Mildred, they wanted me to unpack the things. And then we were going to split.

Mildred: How could they?

Tammy: They got things to do.

Mildred: What of the instruments?

Tammy: They trust you. I think even Tommy trusts you.

Mildred: They have to go to work. I understand that.

Tammy: They don't work. There ain't no work.

Mildred: So why must you leave so soon?

Tammy: I don't know, mam .. Mildred. They just have things to do.

Mildred: I see. What if I paid them to rehearse? Would they be interested in that?

Tammy: We don't want no money for rehearsing.

Mildred: What if I paid you each twenty dollars? That would come to eighty dollars, ten less than ninety dollars.

Tammy: To rehearse?

Mildred: Eighty dollars is a lot for me. It's half a month for me. You wouldn't know about a fixed income, would you Tammy?

Tammy: No, mam.

Mildred: It means that's all there is, there isn't any more. For a whole month. That's my food, my lights, my gas, everything for one month. You see what I mean?

Tammy: I think so.

Mildred: I can't afford to give up that kind of money, except if it's on something really important, like music. Music is important to me .. As important as wheat crackers. More important. Do you think they would be willing to rehearse under those conditions?

Tammy: Conditions?

Mildred: Knowing what I know.' For eighty dollars. Eighty fixed income dollars?

Tammy: I could ask them. (*exits*)

Mildred: I suppose I should have consulted you, Jimmy ole boy. You would have dealt with it more directly. I'm not afraid of them. They're just kids.

Tammy: (*reenters*) They want to know why.

Mildred: Why what?

Tammy: Why you want to pay them.

Mildred: They want the money don't they? Without getting .... problems?

Tammy: Yes. (*she exits*)

Mildred: (*To Jimmy*) Everybody needs a way out, right Jimmy? A chance to make good a mistake? I'll make them pay good. *(looks through the music)* Aha, four part harmony.

Tammy: (*reenters followed by the boys*) They want to know what they have to do.

Mildred: There you are. Who is the tenor?

David: Mam?

Mildred: I need an alto, a tenor, and a baritone. Who sings high?

David: I do.

Mildred: Good. Come here. Sing this.

David: I can't read no music.

Mildred: Then we'll start with Tommy.

Tommy: .Count me out.

Mildred: A music group that can't read music. Oh, well, Bruce. Just follow me. "Lida Rose, I'm home again Rose to put the sun back in the sky".

Mildred and Bruce: "Lida Rose, I'm home again Rose to put the sun back in the sky. "

Mildred: Good. Can you remember that? (he grunts) Well try. Go practice over there. (*He does*) Next.

Mildred: David, now you. "Lida Rose, I'm home again Rose to put the sun back in the sky •.. " (*harmonizes*)

Mildred and David: " Lida Rose I'm home again Rose to put the sun back in the sky •.. "

Mildred: Excellent. I always wanted to work with natural talent. David you find a corner. Can you remember that?

David: I think so.

Mildred: How is it going, Bruce? (*Bruce grunts*) Now, Tommy. Don't be shy. (*Hands him the sheet music*)

Tommy: I'm no good at this.

Mildred: All I ask is an honest effort. With me.

Mildred and Tommy: "Lida Rose, I'm home again Rose to put the sun back in the sky ... " Wonderful. I have talent here. (Tommy moves off) Now, Tammy, you are the counter melody. Come on, I know you can sing.

Mildred: "Sweet and low, sweet and low, dream of a love song that might have been…" Got it? Here are the words. It is from the Music Man, remember?

Tammy: No.

Mildred: My goodness.

Mildred and Tammy: "Sweet and low, sweet and low, dream of a love song that might have been ... "

Mildred: Now we put it all together. Remember your parts? Come on

now. Let's see what we've got. (*They sing their parts*) Bravo! Bravo! What a group. My new group. Better than ever. Except, David, its, .. " to put the sun back in the sky." not "into". O.K., once more for good. (They all sing it again) Perfect. (*clapping*) Now the second line.

Tommy: I got to have a break.

Mildred: We'll break when we've finished this part. Then we'll have a bit of lunch and take on the second verse.

Tommy: I'm taking a break. I got a nicotine fit.

Mildred: We'll break when I say break.

Tammy: Don't mess with him, Mildred.

Mildred: Who is the director here? (*Tommy starts to take out a cigarette*) Another temperamental artist. I thought Arthur was the only one.

Tommy: Who is Arthur? (*Starting to light up*)

Mildred: Don't light that thing in here young man. Jimmy has a lung condition.

Tommy: Who is Jimmy?

David: Jimmy is her husband. He's sick in the back room.

Mildred: He's only deaf, but cigarette smoke makes him sick.

Tommy: Tough titty.

Tammy: Bruce, talk to him. (*Bruce takes him aside and whispers*)

Mildred: It's a quartet that sings it on the stage but ...

Tommy: I don't care what she knows.

Mildred: Now you just come on back, Tommy. The second part starts just the same as the first. "Lida Rose, I'm home again Rose", now it changes a bit, ... " about a thousand kisses shy", then, " Here'is my love song, not fancy of fine, Lida Rose, oh, wont you be mine.!' Come on Tommy. Don't be shy. I know you can do it.

Tommy: I'm not doing it, Bruce. I don't care what she knows.

Tammy: Tommy Tetro!

Mildred: This is your chance to make good a mistake. I believe ...

Tommy: I'm not singing no fruity songs for some old bag!

Mildred: I can always call the police. I know what you did.

Tommy: We didn't steal no money. And you're not calling no goddamn police. (*Goes to the phone and pulls the cord off the wall*)

Mildred: Jimmy! Jimmy! *(races to the back room. and holds her arms behind her back)* Thief. Jimmy!

David: Let go of her.

Tommy: I can't. What do you want me to do?

Mildred: Thief!

Tommy: Shut up. Or I'll break your arm.

Mildred: Owwww!

Tammy: Let go. Now you've done it.

Tommy: Shut up, Tammy.

Tommy: Shut up. (*To David*) Bring that Jimmy out here. I don't want him sneaking out.(*David exits*)

Mildred: You leave Jimmy alone.

Tommy: I said shut up. We didn't steal no money.

Mildred: You think I'm a crazy old lady.

Tommy: I said shut up. Sit down. (*forces her into chair*)

David: (*reenters*) There's noone there

Tommy: He ran out the back.

David: No one has been there.

Mildred: You killed my Jimmy. Murderers, Murderers!!

Tommy: I said shut up. (*grabs cloth and gags her. She struggles and finally goes limp*)

Tommy: A good place to practice, right David?

Bruce: Good grief.

David: Now what?

(Blackout)

ACT II

(Mildred is tied and gagged in an upright chair. She is awake but makes no movement, no struggle. The boys are practicing and Tammy is making baloney sandwiches. The room is a mess.)

Bruce: Ready, from the second verse. 1,2,3,4 ...

Together: *(they sing)* We play on your windshield, we lay rubber for you.

We'll stomp on your dashboard, we'll kill if you sue.

Bruce and David: *(Tommy stops singing)* We'll slash on your tires, we'll zippo your tank.

Bruce: Hold on. *(they stop singing)* What's wrong Tommy~ Where were you?

Tommy: I don't get it.

Bruce: You stopped singing.

Tommy: That," we'll kill if you sue" part. I don't get it.

Bruce: Sure it goes. "We lay rubber for you, We'll kill if you sue." "You" goes with "sue". What's wrong with that?

Tommy: It don't sound right.

Bruce: I don't have no trouble. How about you, Davi d?

David: I don't have no trouble.

Tommy: It don't sound right. "We'll kill if you sue." I can't say it.

Bruce: "We'll kill if you sue, we'll kill if you sue'.' Just practice it a bit.

Tommy: I have practiced it. It don't sound right. It's the "we'll kill" part.

Bruce: What's wrong with it?

Tommy: It don't sound right.

Tammy: (*passing sandwich to Bruce*) Baloney?

Bruce: Not right now.

Tammy: (*offering it to David*) No mustard.

David: We're practicing.

Tammy: It don't sound right.

Bruce: We're working things out.

Tammy: Stinkers! (*starts to take sandwich to Mildred*)

Tommy: She don't get nothing either.

Tammy: Poor Mildred. She's going to starve.

Bruce: She gets fed when we say so.

Tammy: Poor Mildred.

Tommy: Shut up, Tammy.

Tammy: Well, what am I supposed to do with this thing?

Bruce: Eat it, and leave us alone.

Tammy: You make me mad, all of you.

David: What if we say, " We stomp if you sue?"

Bruce: We used "stomp".

Tommy: Use it again.

Bruce: " We'll stomp on your dashboard, we'll stomp if you sue"?

Tommy: What's wrong with that?

Bruce: You can't use it twice.

Tommy: Why not?

David: Bruce is right. You can't use it twice like that.

Tommy: We're punk, we can do what we like.

Bruce: Except you can't use the same word twice in the same line.

Tommy: We used "we" twice.

David: That's different.

Tommy: It's the same word twice.

Bruce: David's right. It's a different thing.

Tammy: Why can't she have a sandwich?

Tommy: Because we said so.

Tammy: She looks so hungry.

Tommy: Tammy, shut up!!

Tammy: Screw off, buddy.

Tommy; I SAID SHUT UP !!!

Tammy: You're not my father.

Tommy: Tell her, Bruce.

Bruce: Shut up, Tammy.

Tammy: You're bastards, all of you.

David: What if we do it, "We hit on your dashboard, we stomp if you sue"?

Bruce: Say it again.

David: "We hit on your dashboard, we stomp if you sue."

Bruce: How about that, Tommy?

Tommy: I like it.

Bruce: Great! Mark it in. (*They take pencils and erase and write on their music*) Okay.

Tommy: (still writing) How do you spell stomp?

Bruce: Tammy?

Tammy: S-T-O-M-P

Bruce: Thank you, Tammy.

Tommy: Thank you, Tammy.

David: Thank you, Tammy.

Tammy: Bastards.

Tommy: I don't like the part where it says, "We lay rubber for you."

David: He doesn't like it because it's my song.

Bruce: What's wrong with that?

David: He doesn't have a reason.

Tommy: It sounds too nice. We're supposed to be bad, and here we are laying rubber for people.

David: That's bad.

Tommy: What's bad about it?

David: You make a lot of noise. You peel out. People don't like that.

Tommy: I like it.

Tammy: It gets on people's nerves.

Tommy: You're getting on my nerves.

Tammy: Screw you, buddy.

Bruce: Take five.

Tommy: Well, she gets on my nerves.

Bruce: I said take five. I mean it. Take five.

Tommy: I'm getting a cigarette.

Tammy: We're all out of cigarettes.

Tommy: Shit.

Bruce: David, why don't you run down and get some cigarettes?

David: Sure. Give me some money.

Tommy: Go get some.

(*David goes to Mildred's envelope and takes out a few bills*)

David: Why don't I get a six pack while I'm at it?

Tommy: Good thinking. (*David takes a few more bills*)

Tammy: We could use mustard.

Tommy: Why mustard?

Tammy: For the baloney, stupid. (*David takes another bill*)

Tommy: (*goes and rips money away from David*) We're not buying no mustard. What do you think, we're rich?

Bruce: (*going to Tommy*) Give me the money. That will stop this fighting.

Tommy: (*handing the money to Bruce*) I got to get out of here. Mildred gives me the creeps. (*Goes to the door*)

David: I'm going to. (*goes to door*)

Bruce: (*following them*) This is a real expedition.

Tammy: Get some mustard, Bruce, will you?

Bruce: Shit, Tammy.

Tammy: We need it.

Bruce: O.K.   (*exits*)

Tommy: (*rentering partially*) And don't feed her nothing.

Tammy: I won't. (*She turns and looks at Mildred who begins to move trying to communicate with her*) Now, don't you move, Mildred. Everything is going to be all right. (*Mildred starts moving somewhat wildly in her chair, her eyes batting back and forth*) Please, Mildred, I said don't move .... What do you want? ... You're going to hurt yourself that way. They shouldn't have left me alone. What do you want? You want a drink of water? (*Mildred stops momentarily*) I can't get you no water, Mildred. I'm not supposed to get you nothing (pause) I'11 get you some water. (*Mildred starts moving again*) You don't want water. I '11 get you something. (*she exits. Mildred sits still*) (*She enters with cocoa tin*) How about some cocoa? *(no response, she exits, continues from offstage)* Cocoa would be good for you. Tommy is not a bad kid. He's wild, and he gets real angry, but he's not bad. (*sticks her head in*) He can't stand being in one place too long. His mother used to hold him over the woodstove to dry his clothes. Sugar? (*exits to get cocoa*) Actually, he's real innocent. (*reenters with cocoa*) He doesn't even know about birth control. Can you believe that? Cocoa? (*Mildred gets wilder*) Come on, Mildred, everybody likes cocoa. (*and wilder*) For me, please ... Well, I can't force you. (*puts cocoa aside, she becomes calm*) You know, you're a lot like Tommy. All jumping around and no action. You know me and Tommy have never gone all the way. Sometimes we don't even get half way ... He's younger than the rest of the kids he goes around with. Younger than David and Bruce and me. Tommy's very insecure. You wouldn't believe that would you, Mildred, the way he acts. That's all puff and show. When we're by ourselves, I can hardly get two words out of him. Sometimes he falls asleep in my arms after we've been making out ... after he's done his thing on my pants or my coat. Yukk! He'll fall asleep just like a baby. Just like my little baby ... You don't want to hear about all this, do you Mildred? Want a baloney sandwich? They're all made except for the mustard. If they forget the mustard, I'll brain them ... You can have some cocoa to wash it down. (*pushes baloney sandwich at her*) No baloney? (*takes it away*) Cocoa and baloney doesn't appeal to you. Me neither. I don't know why you don't get sick with that thing in your mouth. (*Mildred starts to move again*) Mildred, what do you want? Stop it! Please, Mildred! I wish you would stop that. You're going to hurt yourself and die, and we'll catch hell for it. MILDRED! PLEASE! PLEASE!! (*Mildred stops moving*) There, that's better. That's better, Mildred: Now you just be quiet. They should be back soon with the mustard. You just hold on Tommy babysits sometimes with me. He never takes advantage. Jus make out. On the couch, up against the refrigerator. I think he's afraid I'll get pregnant. I'll tell you, he's got a long way to go. Don't those boys talk to each other~ What about Jimmy? He ever take your pants down? You ain't got no children, do you? •. He must have took them down, you were married forever, the way it looks. He must have got them down at least once or twice. Why else would you be calling to him all the time when he isn't here, unless he got them down once in a while? Mildred, I wish you could talk. I tell you, why don't you nod your head? Up and down if he got your pants down, side to side if he didn't. Ready? GO! (*Mildred nods up and down*) I knew it. Jimmy got them down. I knew he did. (*She then nods side to side*) No, he didn't. What are you trying to say? Yes he did and no he didn't. Mildred, you are a queer old bird. (*Mildred gets wild and starts jumping in her chair, struggling and mumbling under her gag*) No, not that again. I asked you, Mildred, not to do that. I can't stand you doing that! Come on, Mildred! (Shaking her) Stop! STOP! (*Mildred slumps over suddenly*) Now what? Mildred, what are you doing? What? Don't die on me! Mildred?! (*Takes off her gag*) Mildred, take this. It's cocoa. It's good for you. Come on, Mildred. Please! (*Mildred comes around, takes a sip as it spills on her*) That's a girl. That's a good girl. (*Mildred gradually comes to a sitting position*).

Mildred: Tammy.

Tammy: There you go, Mildred.

Mildred: Tammy, you're a nice girl. Do me a favor.

Tammy: There is plenty more baloney ...

Mildred: Bring me Tommy's guitar .

Tammy I'll fix you a nice sandwich. No mustard.

Mildred: Just for a minute.

Tammy: I couldn't do that.

Mildred: You know, Tammy, you could be in a lot of trouble ...

Tammy: Tommy'd kill me.

Mildred: It's not every day that an old woman is bound and gagged in her own home ...

Tammy: Tommy doesn't let no one mess with his guitar.

Mildred: ... as nice and sweet as Tommy might be, as kind and considerate he is to you, as misunderstood and cuddily he is on your dates ...

Tammy: Don't ask me, please don't ask me...

Mildred: ... as quiet and passionate he is next to the refrigerator you must know one thing, Tammy, and this is for your own good. It is better for someone to tell you now than after you are married for thirty years.

Tammy: No, Mildred, pleeeease ...

Mildred: ... that as talented, and intelligent, and underrated as your Tommy might be ...

Tammy: Mildred!

Mildred: ... he still can't tune his guitar, and no matter how creative and new your group is, and in spite of all the time and effort that you put into being fresh and innovative, if you continue to play with untuned instruments, no one, not even the dumb hicks that used to to come to hear you play will ever think you know anything about music. Bring me the guitar.

Tammy: I can't do that.

Mildred: You can you do it.

Tammy: I can't untie you. They'd massacre me.

Mildre: You know, Tammy, you could get in a lot of trouble...

Tammy: Mildred, I can't. I don't know how.

Mildred: I'll show you.

Tammy: Oh, Mildred.

Mildred: Noone said life would be easy.

Tammy: (*goes to the guitar and picks it up as if it were hot*) He's going to find out. I know it .... Now what?

Mildred: Put the strap over your shoulder. (*she does*) Now, pluck the top string with your right hand.

Tammy: (*nothing happens*) Oh, I broke it.

Mildred: The power's off. There's a switch. On the top of that box. (*Tammy finds switch, flips it on, the amplifier humms*) There you go.

Tammy: This is scary, Mildred.

Mildred: Now pluck the second string from the top.

Tammy: (*She does*) This one?

Mildred: That's a good girl. That's B. It sounds O.K. (*she plucks it. It is sour*) You Hear that?

Tammy: I think so.

Mildred: Now pluck the second string on the fifth fret.

Tammy: The what on the what ?

Mildred: See the little metal things, yes, there. Now count down five from the top and press your finger hard, good, Tammy. Now play both strings, the top E should sound like the fretted E. *(Tammy tries and they don't)* Now turn the peg for the top string, yes, that one. Make it lower, no the other way,.now it's a little flat, .. just a little sharp,.O.K. how does that sound?

Tammy: I did it, Mildred, I did it!

Mildred: Yes, you did it.　　　(*telephone rings*)

Tammy? Stop! Who's that? Who is it?

(*telephone continues to ring*)

Mildred: Maybe, it's Tommy.

Tammy: No, no. It's for you.

Mildred: I better answer it. They'll think something is wrong.

Tammy: (*putting the guitar down, but not turning it off*) Who will?

Mildred: Busybodies. Neighbors. Whoever is on the phone. I'm always home.

Tammy: (*goes to the phone*) Maybe, it is Tommy. (*picks up receiver*) It's for you. (*shoving the phone at her*) Here, take it. Don't say anything. (*holds receiver for Mildred to talk*)

Mildred: Hi, Betty. (*puts chin over phone*) It's Betty, my neighbor. Her husband is in the hospital. *(to Betty)* It's just one of the kids that play music. (*chin over phone*) Free my hands .. don't worry. (*Tammy unties her hands. Then to Betty*) No, it isn't Arthur. No I'm not imagining it. (*To Tammy*) She thinks I'm a dodo. Harmless, but a dodo. (*Her hands are free and she takes the receiver from Tammy*) No,it isn't Susan or Billy. They are all grown up. Don't you think I know that? *(To Tammy)* Tammy, sing something for Mrs.Maynard.

Tammy: (*in a whisper*) I don't do solos.

Mildred: Something to show Mrs. Maynard that I'm not a dodo. (*To Betty*) No, Betty, I don't accuse you of anything. (*To Tammy*) Try " Lida Rose". (*on phone*) How's Bert? (*covering phone and waving to Tammy*) She doesn't suspect a thing. Just sing something, anything, go! (*To Betty*) How's Bert. That's too bad.

Tammy: (*singing*) Daisy, Daisy give me your answer do… (*etc*)

Mildred: (*at the same time*) ... back in intensive care. I know. I know. Some of the doctor can be brutal ... (*to Tammy*) That song is for a man,dear. (*To Betty*) .... what a way to treat a person, and you his wife...

Tammy: "But you'll look sweet, upon the seat, of a bicycle built for two ... "

Mildred: (*To Tammy*) That part is for a man. (*To Betty*) Yes, she has a fine voice. She doesn't know how to select material yet. (*To Tammy*) I don't have time to transpose it for you now, dear. *(To Betty)* One of those gender problems. She is quite a talent ... totally untrained. (*To Tammy*) Pick another song. Mrs. Maynard thinks you have talent. (*In a whisper*) She doesn't suspect a thing. (*To Betty*) She's making another selection. Maybe, we could get Tammy to go serenade Bert •..

Tammy: (*Having picked up another sheet of music*) "In a canyon, in a cavern, excavating for a mine...

Mildred: Of course, not in intensive care ...

Tammy: Dealt a miner...

Mildred: (*To Tammy*) Dwelt That's dwelt a miner ...

Tammy: Sorry, ... "Dwelt a miner forty-niner and her daughter Clementine."

Mildred: (at the same time) Yes, they have a group ... entertain? .. I suppose so, Betty .. for the hospital society? ...

Tammy: "Oh, my darling, oh, my darling, oh my darling Clementine.

We are lost and gone forever, dreadful sorry, Clementine."

Mildred: ... not intensive care. (*To Tammy*) Do you do benefits?

Tammy: Who?

Mildred: The group. Do you do benefits?

Tammy: (Ishrugs) Drove she ducklings to the water, every morning just at nine. (The boys enter, Tammy sees them) Dah, dee, dah, dah.

Dah, dee, dah, dah, dah, dee, …

Mildred: No, its not rock n' roll .... No, I wouldn't call it that. (*Tommy goes to his instrument*) Oh, no. I'm fine. I'm always my best around young people. (*Mildred sees the boys*) Betty , let me call you back ... (*Hangs up the phone long pause*)

Tommy: Who's been been messing with my guitar?

Bruce: Tammy ... what the hell is going on?

(*blackout*)

SCENE 2

(Mildred is tied up again. She is slumped over. There are beer cans everywhere. Everything is a mess. Tammy is trying to work a tape recorder that the boys have bought with Mildred's money)

Bruce: 1,2,3,4 ... 1,2,3,4 •..

Group: "Going on a dump run, Going to have some dump fun. Going on a dump run, Going to shoot some rats."

Bruce: Hold it! Hold it! Tammy, stop the tape.

Tammy: How do I?

Bruce: Push the stop button.

Tammy: O.K. *(stops tape plays back)*

Bruce: You hear that, David? You're off. It's Boom,whack,whack-whack, Boom, whack,whack-whack: ...

David : Right, Boom ,whack ,whack-whack, Boom whack,whack-whack.

Bruce: You were doing: Boom,whack,whack, Boom whack,whack ... Couldn't you hear it?

David: Not on that dumb thing. Couldn't you get something decent?

Bruce: Not with eighty dollars.

Tommy: It needs speakers.

David: It needs sound. That's what it needs.

Tammy: Mildred's on a fixed income.

Tommy: Nobody's talking to'YOll.

Bruce: Again. 1,2,3,4 .. 1,2,3,4 ...

Group: (as they play Mildred begins to snore)

Going on a dump run, Going to have some dump fun Going on a dump run

Going to shoot some rats."

Bruce: Stop! Stop! (They stop) David, it's Boom, whack ,whack-whack , Boom, whack ,whack-whack. (rewinds the tape)

David: I'm doing Boom, whack, whack,-whack ..•

Bruce: The shit you are.

David: Shit I'm not.

Bruce: Listen! (plays tape)" Going on a dump run

Going to have some dump fun

Going on a dump run (stops tape)

What's that?

Daivid: What's what?

Tamry: I can't hear nothing.

Bruce: Listen! (replays)

Bruce: Mildred' s snoring on the tape.

Tonmy: If we had sane decent speakers you could hear the snoring.

Tammy: I heard it.

Bruce: (to Tammy) Tell Mildred to stop snoring. She's messing up the tape.

Tammy: (to Mildred) Stop snoring, Mildred.

Bruce: Tell her so she can hear you.

Tammy: I don't want to wake her. She's real tired.

Tommy: She's tired?

Bruce: I am tired. She's snoring on the tape. Tell her.

Tammy: Mildred? (shakes her)

Tommy: Tell her to give us the dough for some speakers while you're at it.

Tammy: Haven't you done enough?

Tommy: No, I ain't done enough. (goes to desk for envelope) Mildred has not done enough. Tammy, your job is to keep her from snoring and not telling us what is enough when it ain't enough. (looking in envelope) There aint enough here for a sixpack. She must have some more put away somewhere. (rummages in the drawers)

Tammy: She's on a fixed income.

Tommy: What the hell does that mean?

Tammy: She gets one check a month.

Tommy: I ain't waiting in this dump no month. We need cash now.

Tammy: She ain't got any.

Bruce: Come on, Tommy, let's tape this and get going.

Tammy: You can't leave her, Bruce.

Bruce: Why not?

Tammy: What if she needs to go to the bathroom?

Bruce: I won't stop her.

Tammy: You can't do that.

Bruce: Why not? This place smells already.

Tammy: You can't, that's all.

Bruce: It's not my problem.

David: Bruce is a recording artist.

Tommy: He ain't no artist without no speakers. (exits to bedroom)

Tammy: He ain't no artist, no way.

David: She insulted you, Bruce.

Bruce: While we're gone, Tammy is going to look after Mildred.

Tammy: I'm not doing anymore babysitting.

David: Remember what happened last time.

Bruce: It won't happen again, will it, Tammy?

Tammy: I'm not taking no orders from noone.

Tommy: (*reenters carrying a gold watch*) Look at this. We could get something for this.

Tammy: That's Jimmy's watch.

Tommy: Jimmy is dead.

Tammy: Then it belongs to Mildred.

Tommy: Mildred. Who is Mildred? Some old lady who don't know her husband is dead.

Tammy: She knows he's dead.

She just won't admit it. Why should she?

Tommy: What does she care about some old watch? What difference does it make now? Let's split.

Tammy: I'm not staying with her.

Tommy: We got to hock a watch and buy some speakers.

David: That's men's work.

Tammy: What would you know about work? All of you.

Bruce: You can't cut a record without decent speakers.

Tommy: If you can't hear some old lady snoring?

Tammy: I heard her. I heard her all right. Let Mildred go, Bruce. Before something bad happens.

Bruce: Someone has to set priorities. Right now, number one in priorities is getting some decent speakers.

Tommy: Come on, let's split.

Tammy: I ain't no thief.

Tommy: You ain't no thief. I ain't no thief. Who are you then?

Tammy: I'm not your girlfriend no more.

Tommy: That's fine with me.

Bruce: (*They move to the door*) Come on, Tommy.

David: (*exiting*) "I ain't no thief. You ain't no thief. I'm growing up and turning a leaf." How about that, Tommy?

Tommy: (*exiting*) It sucks.

Tammy: (*stands looking at Mildred. Runs to the door*) Wait for me!

(*they have left*) Shoot! (*Goes back, gathers her stuff, starts to leave. She looks at Mildred, puts down her things, goes to the kitchen, returns with bread and water, tries to set it up so Mildred can feed herself without luck*)

Mildred: (*begins to wake up*)

Tammy: Wake up. Mildred. Please, Mildred. I can't stand it any longer. You have to drink something. You will starve yourself. Wake up! (*Takes the gag out of her mouth*) I'm going home. You'll have to take care of yourself. I don't care if they get angry with me. I got to get out of here.

Mildred: Water.

Tammy: (*Letting her drink*) Good, Mildred, water is good for you.

Mildred: The bathroorn. I have to pee. Untie me.

Tammy: No tricks.

Mildred: No tricks.

Tammy: (*Unties her feet*) I broke up with Tommy ... While you were sleeping. Tommy is not a bad boy. I know it's hard for you to see his good side. He has to act tough in the group. It's the punk music. Some of it is bound to rub off. *(She helps her up and to the bathroom offstage)* He wouldn't have taken Jimmy's watch if the band had more money.

Mildred: Jimmy's watch?

Tammy: A band always needs new equipment. Even I heard you snoring without no speakers.   We always need new speakers. It's part of being a band.

Mildred: Jimmy's gold watch?

Tammy: A good pair of speakers cost a lot of money. They'll get used speakers. I was thinking of breaking up with Tommy before ...

Mildred: I need some toilet paper. In the cupboard in the hall.

Tammy: He does have a terrible temper.

Mildred: (*Makes a break for it, rushing back on stage, waddling in her drawers*) Jimmy! Jimmy! Jimmy!

Tammy: MILDRED! (*rushes in carrying the toilet paper, catches Mildred as she reaches the door*) I said NO! You promised me,Mildred! (*drags her back to the seat and ties her feet*) You gave me your word. Mildred! Why can't I trust you? What's wrong with you? Jimmy is dead. Don't you understand? Jimmy is dead!

Mildred: Jimmy is my light man. I need my light man. I held him. I rocked him. He was just skin and bones. Something gave way inside his gut. (*reliving*) The cramps. I can't stop the cramps. I'll rub them out. I can't stop the cramps. I only have two hands. I won't let you go. I shouldn't have rocked you so hard. You were just skin and bones. The disease ate you up and then something gave way. Your beautiful legs were tied up in knots. I'll stay with you. I'll call the family. There was no family. Just the sheep and the goat. I'll call them in to watch you go. We sold the sheep. We ate the goat. Just relax. The cramps will go away. Just be quiet. Please, Jimmy. He wouldn't. He cried to me, "Let me go, let me go." I never understood that. Please, Jimmy. Just rest. Just relax. Just rest.

Tammy: (*after a long pause*) Tommy took the watch. I'm breaking up with him. I'm sick of him. (*long pause*) The group doesn't really want to be famous. We just want our friends to like us. Everybody hates our music. Bruce says that's a sign that we're getting good.

Mildred: I'm hungry.

Tammy: Have some bread. Do you want some butter? Do you want jam? I'll get you some jam.

Mildred: A little marmalade. It's on the shelf. Behind the stove.

Tammy: I like marmalade. (*exits happily. The telephone rings. She reenters concerned*) The phone. Who is it?

Mildred: Neighbors. Busybodies.

Tammy: Tell them not to call here anymore. (*untieing her hands*)

Mildred: I can't do that. They will come here to see if I'm all right.

Tammy: (*Hands her the phone*) Do something!

Mildred: (*takes the phone*) Oh , hi, Betty .... Oh, I'm fine. ,. No, I'm just a little hoarse ... No, I don't need a thing ... Tammy gets me everything I need ...

Tammy: No, Mildred. (*waving her hands at the mention of her name*)

Mildred: Yes, that's Tammy that you hear. She is so modest. She's a perfect joy, as well as a talent ... Yes, there are boys, too. Bruce,

Tammy: Noooo!

Mildred: David, and Tommy ,,, You know the Hutchins boys, over from Hatch Hill. They are such helpful young people ... No, we don't give young people all the credit that they deserve .... and so talented. Yes, I remember ... the Hospital Society. (*a car approaches, Tammy goes to the door to look*) Yes ... I remember ... yes ... we will need some publicity. (*Tammy returns anxiously motioning for Mildred to finish the conversation*) yes ... Friday at eight. I don't see why not .... Of course, they practice, I'll call to confirm. How is Bert? Comatose, again? Oh, my. (*Tammy giving her wild signal to hangup finally gives the cut signal with her finger on her throat*) Sorry, Betty. I'll have to hang up. We're killing the sheep today. (*hangs up*)

Tammy: (*worried*) I don't want you calling anymore.

Mildred: Betty called me. She always calls me. I don't like it any better than you do.

Tammy: Then stop it.

Mildred: Her husband is very sick. She is a very needful person.

Tammy: She'll only get us in trouble.

Mildred: Us?

Tammy: Tommy will come back. I will get into trouble. Something will happen. Someone will get hurt. My mother will find out. The cops will come.

Mildred: You are frightened.

Tammy: (*Burst into tears*) I told my mom I was at a slumber party. That was two weeks ago.

Mildred: Maybe, you should go home. I didn't think you were here against your will.

Tammy: I can't go home. They will hurt you. I know they will.

Mildred: I can take care of myself, Tammy. Just tie me up and leave me. I'll handle the boys in my own way.

Tammy: No.

Mildred: No what?

Tammy: I am not going. You don't know them.

Mildred: Tammy, they need my help ... Tommy, Bruce, David. Don't you listen to them?

Tammy: Sure I listen.

Mildred: They can't hold their parts. Their harmony is rotten. Not rotten, it just needs some coaching. If they would only give me a chance to help them.

 Mildred: your age. tie me up.

Tammy: Mildred, you're impossible. (*car door slams outside*)

Tammy, I am seventy-four years old. I am five times If I don't know music by now, I'll never learn. Now (*Tammy ties her hands*).

Tammy: Mildred, I must say you are different.

MIldred: Hurry up. I don't want you to get in trouble over poor Mildred. Besides, I have a surprise for you. (*Tammy puts the gag over her mouth so the following is garbled*) I got you a gig.

Tammy: What? (*removing the gag*)

Mildred: I got you a gig. (*Tammy replaces the gag just as the boys enter*)

Tommy: (carrying big box) Hey, babes, we got the speakers. *(blackout)*

SCENE 3

(The set is messier than ever, if that is possible. There sre two big speakers. Tommy is at at the tape recorder; Bruce on piano; David on drums; Mildred sleeping and looks awful)

Tommy: "Death is for the dying."

 Chorus: Death. OOOOH. Death OOOH.!!

 Tommy: "Death is for the dying."

 Chorus: Death, OOOH. Death OOOH.

Tommy: "Death is for the dying."

Chorus:"OOH. OOOH. Death."

Tommy: Death is for the dying

 Bruce: It changes, Tommy. It changes. Isn't it, "Life is for the living"? Then we sing," Life. OOOH. Life. OOOH." Remember?

Tommy: I like it my way.

Bruce: It don't progress, Death is for the dying".

Tommy: I like it.

Bruce: It don't accumulate.

David: It don't go no where.

Tommy: Death don't go nowhere. Am I not correct?

Bruce: The song is boring.

Tammy: It's dumb.

Tommy: I like it. It's my song. Its highly simplified, just like death You can shut up, Tammy.

Tammy: I'm not talking to you.

Tommy: Then don't. It accumulates great. I get a real strong feeling from the words.

Bruce: It weighs on me.

David: It's depressing.

Tammy: It makes me want to puke.

Tommy: I said shut up, Tammy. The song has meaning for me. That's why I wrote it the way I did.

David; What is the meaning?

Tommy: It's about death.

Bruce: Remember how you wrote it first. "Life is for the living.."

Tommy: I remember the old way. I'm not stupid.

David: I liked it that way.

Tommy: But I changed it.

Bruce: The old way made for variety.

Tommy: I changed my mind.

Tammy: What mind?

Tommy: *(raising his fist and taking a step toward her)* I'm going to belt you.

Tammy: You can't. I'm not going with you anymore.

Mildred: (*groans*)

Tammy: Look what you did, you woke Mildred up.

Tommy: Fuck, Mildred.

Tammy: Bruce, tell him to shut up. You watch your language around Mildred. Mildred is a lady, not scum. Bruce, you tell him.

Tommy: I'm going to slug her, Bruce, If she don't shut up. Mildred is a crazy old witch. I hope she dies.

Tammy: If she dies, you killed her. Its your fault, all of you.

Mildred: (*groans*)

Tammy: I'll tell them you killed her.

Tommy: You're in on this. You're just as bad.

Tammy: I give her water.. I take her to the bathroom: one and two. It's all your fault. I hope they send you to the electric chair.

Tommy: Shit, she won't die. She's just crazy. She should be tied up.

Tammy: She's an old lady. She could die at any minute. It would be your fault.

Tommy: Let's get out of here. I'm sick of practicing.

Tammy: If you go Tommy, Tetro, I'm letting Mildred go. I'm taking her out of here, before she dies.

Tommy: I guess we'll have to tie you up too. (*Goes after her*)

Tammy: Let go of me! Bruce! David! Get him off of me! (*The struggle wakes up Mildred who starts to struggle too*)

Bruce: (*grabs Tommy*) O.K., Tommy, cut it out. Help me, David.

(*David is totally ineffective in his efforts, but Tommy separates the m*)

Tammy: I'm calling the cops. Tommy, you've had it.

Tommy: Shut her up. She's ruining the goddamn rehearsal. She's a disruptive influence on the band.

Bruce: Tommy, go out to the car.

Tommy: I ain't going nowhere.

Bruce: (*grabs him and forces him towards the door*) David, help me.

Tommy: Give me the keys. I'll go. Just give me the keys. (*He exits followed by Bruce and David*).

Tammy: (*Going to Mildred and starting to untie her*) Mildred, are you all right?

Mildred: (*groans*)

Tammy: Mildred, I'm getting you out of here. I am through with Tommy. I won't be his mother no more. You shouldn't fight with someone you love and respect. He's got to grow up and not rely on me so much. One person can't expect so much from one other person. It isn't fair. Is it, Mildred? (*finishes untying her*) Come on, we're getting out of here.

(*Reenter Bruce and David. They stand observing near the door*)

Mildred: I'm not going anywhere. This is my house.

Tammy: You'll die here, Mildred.

Mildred: I'm ready for death.

Tammy: I won't let you die, Mildred. I just won't let you. I would feel so bad.

Mildred: (*seeing Bruce and David*) Tammy, I told you something wrong about Jimmy.

Tammy: Jimmy is dead. We know that.

Mildred: I told you wrong. Jimmy didn't die with me. I came home. Something wasn't right. It was so quiet. The sheep always would baa when I came up to the house. They must be in the back pasture. They weren't in the back pasture. They were right in the barn. Jimmy had brought them up with a pail of grain. The grain was on the ground. The sheep were on the ground. He had shot them. He shot the sheep, even the lambs. He shot the chickens too. There were only two chickens but he shot them. Even the cats. They were all his children, all dead and bloody. Then he shot himself. Jimmy was down next to the sheep in the sheep poop, dead. (*pause*) I'm not going anywhere. I'm staying right here.

Tammy: (*goes to the phone*) I'm calling the cops.

Bruce: What are you doing?

Tammy: I'm calling the cops. (*telephone rings*) That was quick. (*she starts to answer but Bruce holds the receiver down*) It's the telephone.

Bruce: I can hear it.

Tammy: It's Mildred's nosey neighbors. You got to answer it. They'll come here if you don't. They'll get worried. Don't worry, you can trust Mildred.

Bruce: (*handing the phone to Mildred*) Come on, David, let's practice. (*goes to piano*)

Mildred: Yes, Betty .. Of course, Betty, No, I'm just a little dry. (*Tammy hands her a glass of water*) There, is that better? ... No, I don't want you to come over. (*turning to others*) She wants to come over.

Bruce: No way. (*He has lost interest in Mildred. He plays chords*)

Mildred: No, really, Betty. I am fine... Yes, they are here.

David: Who's here?

Tammy: We are, stupid.

David: How does that lady know?

Mildred: Well, they're not practicing just this moment.

David: What does she know?

Tammy: Everything.

David: Everything?

Bruce: (*in a daze*) She wasn't supposed to be on the phone.

David: I need a beer. (*opens a beer*)

Tammy: This place is a mess. (*goes about straightening*)

Mildred: Yes, they are sitting around drinking cocoa. Naturally, they like cocoa. (*hand on phone*) Betty is surprised you like cocoa. She thinks you drink beer. (*back on the phone*) I fix it like I always fix it. I don't tell the mothers. Its awful on the teeth, but its great on the vocal chords ... (*hand on phone*) She wants to bring us more cocoa. I think she really wants to hear us rehearse.

Bruce: No way.

David: Tell her our rehearsals are closed.

Tammy: So are the concerts.

Mildred: (*hand on phone*) She wants some pictures. She wants to bring her camera.

Bruce: (*playing chords*) What for?

Mildred: Publicity.

David: Publicity?

Tammy: These ashtrays are filthy.

Tommy: (*enters*) Bruce, give me the keys.

Tammy: Smoking is a filthy habit.

Tommy: Mildred's on the the phone.

Bruce: Tell her we don't want no publicity.

David: Publicity means newspapers.

Tommy: Who's on the phone?

Tammy: Betty.

David: And newspapers mean cops.

Mildred: She wants a feature story for the Sunday paper.

Bruce: No way.

Tommy: Who is Betty? Mildred ain't tied up.

David: I don't want no camera here.

Tammy: She hasn't been tied up for five minutes.

Tommy: Camera?

Bruce: Betty wants to take pictures.

Tommy: Of who?

Tammy: Of us stupid.

Tommy: NO WAY! NO WAY!

David: They'll call the cops. I'm getting out of here.

Bruce: David, why don't you work on your Boom, wack, wack-wack, Boom?

Tommy: We got to get rid of Mildred.

David: I know my Boom, wack ,wack-wack. I am not stupid. (*He starts to pack up his stuff)* I'm packing.

Tammy: You finished with this? (*holds beer can up for David, shakes it, puts it back on the table, Bruce sings*)

Mildred: I can't hear you, Betty. They are thrashing out some new lyrics.

Tommy: As I see it we have two choices. We kill her or leave her here to die.

Mildred: Sorry, Betty, just an interruption.

Tommy: I say we kill her.

Tammy: Does anybody want soggy chips before I heave them?

David: I don't want to go to jail.

Mildred: Ja .. el, David. Remember, now. Sorry, Betty.

Bruce: We stink ... We don't smell, we're just plain bad.

Mildred: David never remembers it's "get a little drunk and you land in ja..el. He always says"jail". Only Perry Como sings it that way. Perry Como is too jazzed up for me.

Tommy: Nobody will miss the old bag.

Bruce: "We play on your windshield, we lay rubber for you We hit on your dashboard, we'll stomp if you sue .... " I have a rhythm note for you David.

Tammy: You could use a shave, David.

Tommy: I tell you nobody's going to miss one old lady. Who would suspect a punk band?

Mildred: It's noisy in here. So much creativity

Maybe I should call you back.

Bruce: I changed your copy, David. It's, "stomp if you sue".

David: Whos helping me with my drum case?

Tammy: (*enters*) I'm not cleaning the bathroom, it stinks in there.

David: Listen, I'm going to need help.

Tommy: We kill her and put her in the drum set.

David: Not my drum set.

Tammy: I'm taking the mustard with me. Mildred, I said I'm taking the mustard.

Mildred: I'll talk to you later. Yes, send all the reporters you can.

David: No reporters.

Bruce: We need some new harmonies.

Tommy: (*in Mildred's ear*) Lady, you're dead, lady.

Mildred: I'm hanging up now, Betty.

Tammy: There is a mess in the bathroom.

David: My drum set is my castle.

Mildred: I said I am hanging up! (*slams phone*) Busybody!

Tommy: I say kill Mildred.

Bruce: We need new rhythms.

David: The keys, Bruce, the keys.

Tammy: I'm not cleaning no bathroom mess.

I Mildred: (*sings*) "There is someone I am longing to see ...

Tommy: I say kill her.

Tammy: (*brushing by Tommy*) You're in the way.

Mildred: "I hope that he ... "

David: I need the keys, Bruce.

Mildred: "Turns out to be ... "

Bruce: Boom, wack, wack-wack, Boom .

Mildred: "Someone to watch over me . "

Tommy: Lady, you are dead.

Tammy: (*to Tommy*) Be nice to Mildred. They know we're here.

Tommy: Who knows.

Tammy: The whole world.

Mildred: (*with force*) "I'm a little Lass whose lost in the wood

Tommy: You're on my shit list.

Mildred and Tammy: "I know I could, always be good ...

(*David picks up Tommy's guitar, strums; Bruce and he begin to accompany the singing*)

Tommy: You can't even sing.

M&T: " To the one who'll watch over me .•.. (*David and Bruce in full accompaniment*) I know you may not be the man some girls think of as handsome, but to my heart you carry the key   "

Tommy: Stop it Tammy. I'm warning you.

M&T: (*arm in arm*)"Won't you please to tell him, put on some speed,

 Tommy: You've had it.

M&T: " Follow my lead, Oh how I need, someone to watch over me." (*long drum roll, they embrace*)

Mildred: You are a sweetheart.

Tommy: Fuck youl Fuck all of you! (*goes on a rampage knocking over the equipment*)

David: Stop it, Tommy.

Bruce: Stop it.

Tammy: Stop him.

 Bruce: (*grabbing him*) What are you doing?

Tommy: Let go of me. Are you crazy?

 David : (*Going after Tommy*) The creep broke my high hat. I'll kill him!

Tommy: Mildred's made a bunch of pansies out of all of you. What's wrong with you?

Tammy: What's wrong with you?

Tommy: (*going after Tammy*) I'll kill you. (The*y grab him again*)

Mildred: (*in a booming voice that shocks all of them*) SHUT UP! Excuse me, be quiet! I have had enough. Tammy, help me up._

Tammy: With pleasure.

Mildred: (*stands on shaky legs*) I learned my lesson with Arthur. You can't let artists, and excuse me, I do call musicians artists; you can't let little Arthur's get their own way. There are more important things to life. (*she wobbles and Tammy comes and supports her elbow*) Thank you, Tammy. I don't mean to speak loudly around young girls, but I am angry. You are losers, all of you. Who can rehearse with all this noise? David, throw that beer can away. Cocoa with extra sugar. You have heard it all before but you can't argue with success. Dentists have to make a living, too. But dentists don't know a damn thing about music. Except Andy Williams. No, I am wrong, Perry Como. He was a barber. It's the same damn thing. A little sugar never hurt anybody. I just don't want to take any more foolishness. You understand me, Tommy? You'd better. We have a show to put together and there is not much time. (*Going to the cocoa pan*).

Tommy: What is she talking about?

Mildred: I said SHUT UP, Tommy! The reporters will be here and they will want to see our program. We'll have to have programs printed. We don't even have a program. I have put myself out on a limb with

a lot of important people. (*handing the pot to Tammy*) Tammy, you take the cocoa. (*she rummages through her sheet music*) Yes ... Yes .. Yes.

Tommy: She is nuts.

David: Tommy!

Mildred: There you go, David. You can solo on this one. Here Bruce, take this. I am not nuts. You'll need to transpose I just have priorities. Make it with milk, not water, Tammy. Jimmy is not here. I am sorry about Jimmy. Jimmy is gone. Jimmy is dead. Arthur, Susan, Mary, and Billy are gone. I should know that. I guess I forgot. I shouldn't have kept you here so long without calling your parents. I guess I am a selfish old lady. I apologize for having so little to spend on sound equipment, but a fixed income is a fixed income. I am sorry I couldn't find a better hall for us to play in. The hospital theater is not the best for sound, but this our first gig.

Tommy: Gig?

Mildred: Yes, gig. That's musicians talk,Tommy. I am sorry You have such a limited appreciation for the way we work. I don't rule out your ability to grow with the rest of the group. Now,I want to speak with Tommy alone. Take five. (*all exit except for Tommy*) Tommy I know you don't like me.

Tommy: (*grunts*)

Mildred: You think I'm a crazy old lady ..• Well? Well? Say Something.

Tommy: You're nutty as a hird's pie.

Mildred: I was right. I thought so. So what?

Tommy: Nothing what.

Mildred: Let me explain.

Tommy: What for? Why for? Who cares?

Mildred: I care ... Why crazy? Why Jimmy?

Tommy: Why everything?

Mildred: First Jimmy. Let me tell you about Jimmy.

Tommy: Who cares?

Mildred: I didn't tell this to the others. He was my Jimmy, you

know. You have his watch. You had his watch ... Thase are good
speakers, Tommy .. Better than any gold watch. Jimmy would have
liked those speakers ... Nifty. Jimmy was a lot like you. He had a great
voice. He had a good voice. Why do I play those old songs if not for
Jimmy?

Tommy: Jimmy is dead.

Mildred: Jimmy is dead. But what a voice Jimmy had ... Deep ... He
could sing "Ja .. el" and never quiver, never gulp off the note. He could
sustain. Oh, how Jimmy could sustain, until the end, he could sustain.
Do you understand?

Tommy: (grunts)

Mildred: We played all over. Not just hospital benefits,either.We
played at church suppers. We could draw a crowd, keep a crowd. Oh,
those bean supper crowds. Then one day…

 Tommy: He dropped dead.

Mildred: It was me, Tommy. It wasn't him. It was me.

Tommy: You're nuts.

 Mildred: I had a stroke at fifty-two. Half my side was paralyzed.
Jimmy didn't let me go. He cared for me. Nursed me. He used to say, "
You'll be back in no time, Mill." He called me Mill.

Tommy: Right.

Mildred: But by the time I was better, his voice was gone. No practice.
He tried and tried to get it back. It hurt him so. It was his only joy ...

after we sold the sheep. He waited until I was on my feet again. I could play piano for him but he wouldn't even try. He couldn't reach his low note and he was darned if he would sing like a dentist. One night I played for him. He just sat and rocked in his chair. He went to bed early ... took off his gold watch, your gold watch, and went to bed. In the morning he was gone. I found him all curled up in the bed. (*cries*)

Tommy: (*long pause and then meekly*) You poisoned Tammy against me.

Mildred: If I did, I didn't mean to. Directors are awful people, the pits, but they are necessary.

Tommy: (*pause then in a whisper*) O.K., Mildred.

Mildred: What was that, Tommy?

Tommy: O.K., all right ,already. Can I go?

Mildred: Rehearsal in five minutes. (*he exits*) Not great, but it will do.

(blackout)

Lily Christine as Tammy, 2008

SCENE 4

(*We hear the sound of the piano and of singing before the lights come up. Mildred is on the piano, David on drums, the others around piano*)

Tommy: "Oh sweet and lovely, lady be good ... "

Chorus: "Oh, lady be good ..."

Tommy: "To me. I am so awfully misunderstood ... " (*lights come up*)

Chorus: "Oh, lady be good ..• "

Tommy: "To me."

Chorus: "Bum-de-bum-de-bum"

Tommy: "Oh , please have some pity .• '.'(*voice cracks*) I can't sing this dumb song.

Mildred: Take it from, "Bum-de-bum-de-dum •. "

Chorus: "Bum-de-bum-de-bum ..• "

Tommy: "Oh, please have some pity ...

Chorus: "Bum-de-bum-de-bum ..• "

Tommy: "I'm all alone in this big city .... "

Chorus: "I tell you ..• "

 Tommy: " I am so awfully misunderstood. Oh, lady be ....

(*stops*) Where were you guys? (*Throwing down music*)

I quit. Who wants this hospital gig anyway?

Bruce: Cut the crap, Tommy.

Tommy: It's your dumb fault. Can't you sing backup? What's wrong with you idiots?

David: Shut up, Tommy.

Tommy: Who are you telling to shut up?

Tammy: Shut up, Tommy.

Tommy: (*grabs her arm*) Goddamn, you bitch.

Bruce: Cut it out, Tommy. Let her go.

Mildred: LET! GO! (*he does, then mildly*) Tommy! Take it from, " I tell you".

Tammy: Tell him to keep his hands off me, Mildred.

Mildred: Keep your hands off her, Tommy. And chorus, shape up. This is our last rehearsal. Give Tommy some support, eh.

Tommy: Right, give Tommy some support.

David: I'll give you a break.

Tommy: You just try it.

Give me a break.

Mildred: Shut up! If you can't work together, tie me and gag me, steal my money, and forget about the hospital gig, but I can't take all this bickering!

David: Sorry, Mildred.

Bruce: Sorry, Mildred.

Tammy: Sorry, Mildred.

Tommy: Sorry, Mildred.

Mildred: Apologies accepted. You can see that this is the best way out ... the only way out.

All together: Thank you, Mildred.

Mildred: From the top ...

Tommy: "I am so awfully misunderstood ••. "

Chorus: "Oh, lady be good, to me."

 Mildred: (*clapping*) Bravo!

(*Blackout*)